VENEZIA CONTEMPORANEO DENNIS OPPENHEIM

DENNIS OPPENHEIM

Texts by
Germano Celant
Dennis Oppenheim

CHARTA

Design
Gabriele Nason

Editorial coordination
Emanuela Belloni

Cover design
Studio Camuffo, Venezia

Press office
Silvia Palombi Arte & Mostre,
Milano

Translations
Mark Eaton per Scriptum, Roma

Production
Amilcare Pizzi Arti grafiche,
Cinisello Balsamo, Milano

Color separations
Fratelli Colombo, Milano

Binding
LeGo Service, Cologno Monzese,
Milano

Cover
Upper Cut, 1992

Back cover
Device to Root out Evil, 1996

© 1997
Edizioni Charta, Milano

Illustrations copyright ©
Dennis Oppenheim

His text copyright ©
Germano Celant

All rights reserved

ISBN 88-8158-127-2

Edizioni Charta
via Castelvetro, 9 - 20154 Milano
tel. 39-2-33.60.13.43/6
fax 39-2-33.60.15.24

Printed in Italy

Dennis Oppenheim

Marghera, Industrial area
Pilkington - SIV building
June 15 -October 12, 1997

Comune di Venezia
Assessorato alla Cultura
e allo Spettacolo
Civici Musei Veneziani

Mayor
Massimo Cacciari

Councillor
Gianfranco Mossetto

Director, Musei Civici
Giandomenico Romanelli

Structure Director
Antonio De Marchi

VENEZIA CONTEMPORANEO

Scientific Coordination
Germano Celant
Giandomenico Romanelli

with the Patronage of

Ente Autonomo
La Biennale di Venezia

with the support of
PRADA

with the contribution of
CHARTA

*and with the technical
cooperation of*

PILKINGTON

*Scientific Curators of the
exhibition*
Germano Celant with
Giandomenico Romanelli

Coordination
Sandro Mescola

Staging
Daniela Ferretti
with Piervincenzo Rinaldi

Organization
Angela Fiorella

Design
Studio Camuffo, Venezia

Press Office
Assessorato alla Cultura
e allo Spettacolo
Studio Esseci
Edizioni Charta

Thanks are due to
Maurizio Nardi,
Stefano Poli,
Peter Ryan,
Massimo Venuda,
La Tre P

For their generous contributions to the exhibition and the monograph
published on it's occasion my gratitude to:
For her *Appreciation* and *Belief* Ginny Williams, Denver, Colorado who
permitted "Device to Root Out Evil" to become a reality, for her *Cheerfulness*
Dianne Perry Vanderlip, Denver Art Museum, for his *Compassion* Stefan
Stux, New York, for their *Cooperation* Martin Kottering, Städtische Galerie
Nordhorn and Lewis I. Sharp, Denver Art Museum, for his *Concentration*
Stefano Poli, Venezia, for their *Considerateness* Bernard and Simone
Guttman, Brussel, for his *Devotion* Piervincenzo Rinaldi, Firenze, for his
Exactitude Massimo Venuda, Venezia, for his *Forgiveness Fortitude*
Graciousness and *Inspiration*, Germano Celant, Genova, for their *Integrity*
and *Kindness* Mr. and Mrs. Joseph Helman, New York, for her *Patience*
Leemour Pelli, New York, for *Perseverance* The Joseph Helman Gallery, New
York, for her *Steadfastness* and *Thoughtfulness*, Paris Murray, New York, for
her *Thoroughness* Beth Wilson, New York, for his *Virtuosity*, Drew Cliness,
New York, for her *Wizardry* Amy Plumb, New York.

Dennis Oppenheim

"Venezia Contemporaneo" is the first proof of Venice City Council's desire to be present on the contemporary visual arts scene by permanently involving its municipal museums.

This takes two forms: its participation in the Foundation for the Museum of Contemporary Art, established in association with nine major private collectors in 1996, and the existence not only of an historic basis but also of new stimuli for contemporary creativity in the region and society of Venice, formerly in the old city centre and today in the rapidly changing industrial areas on the mainland. These are the two elements that have influenced us in planning "Venezia Contemporaneo".

Like the collectors who are making their collections available, we wanted to offer the new Foundation the first results of two researches promoted by the Department for Culture and Municipal Museums: the research on Venice's role in contemporary life from the Fifties to the Sixties and the photographic research project on the transformation of the Marghera area.

The exhibitions based on these researches - "L'Officina del contemporaneo" at the Fortuny, and "Venezia-Marghera" at the Pilkington S.I.V. - present a selection of the extensive material collected to date, which is destined for the museum.

"Venezia Contemporaneo", however, is also a re-presentation and a re-consideration of the traditional relationship between Venice and contemporary culture, in which it was contemporary culture that came to Venice (symbolically in the Biennale), over a one-way bridge from the mainland to the historic centre of the city.

The novelty is that this relationship has been reversed. The roots and enzymes of innovation are no longer in the lagoon. The contemporary scene - on earth and water - lies in Marghera, in its historic vestiges, but also and above all in its current potential. Not dead stones but living factories and people.

The bridge now leads in the opposite direction, from Anselm Kiefer at the Museo Correr to Dennis Oppenheim at Marghera, from the upheaval of European tradition - which, however, is deeply-rooted in Europe - to pure American post-industrial creativity. It departs from Venice and arrives at Marghera.

It is therefore the complete symbol of a process of transition that has not yet been completed, and whose completion is the truly political, social and creative challenge Venice must face over the next few years. A foreseen challenge that Venice can win, as is evident from the great enthusiasm and faith shown by a world-famous artist like Oppenheim, who has accepted to experiment with the outcome by constructing and presenting his works in a fully operating factory in Marghera.

"Venezia Contemporaneo" has been realized under the patronage of Ente Autonomo La Biennale di Venezia, with the support of Prada, the contribution of Charta and the technical cooperation of Pilkington S.I.V. Our thanks to all artists who joined in the project with enthusiasm and to the professionalism of all staff of the Department for Culture and Spectacle and the Venice Municipal Museums.

Gianfranco Mossetto
Councillor for Culture, Venice City Council

Contents

Oppenheim's Suspense

Germano Celant

The initial impression is one of suspense. Dennis Oppenheim captures the attention and the participation through a series of events, based on the notion of multiplicity and ambiguity. He adopts a system of refractions which make us lose the sense of reality and displace experience, almost as if he wanted to keep himself at a certain distance, an objective distance both from the things used and from the narrative constructed. Since the Sixties, all his work has centred on the weak and vulnerable points of artistic control, almost as if he wanted to exalt the capacity for survival and the permeability of behaviours towards the absolute formulations of art. In his journey since 1967, all roads cross, the route is labyrinthine and never reaches a central point. It always begins from scratch, from a potential catastrophe of acquired certainties. It is no coincidence that many works, from *Rocked Circle* (1967) to *Predictions* (1972), from *Attempt to Rise Hell* (1974) to *Device to Root Out Evil* (1997), concern the idea of the risk of disaster and of deviant action, which arrives at the physical subversion of the image, as person or icon. In reality it is not clear where the events or things are normal and where they become paranoiac and develop behaviours whose permanence is improbable and casual, schizoid and unexpected.

His itinerary is tortuous and disturbing, it moves in circular and parabolic lines that run from one point to another, rarely returning to the point of departure. His journey, in fact, is one of dispersion and displacement, it tends towards a loss of centre. It marks the loss of a certain answer, almost as if it were a science fiction story that works through the mechanisms of tension in order to reach a climax.

Many works, in fact, are based on a series of surprises, structured according to a rhythm, through identical narrative passages. Nothing is offered calmly, everything is loaded with tension and aggression – it is to be taken in, digested and filtered, from *Digestion* (1994) to *Color Mix* (1995), as the macroscopic evidence of a crisis in the relations between things and beings, between words and images. Oppenheim pushes associations and contents to their limit, combining objects and plants, bodies and materials, gestures and writing, with a Duchamp-like mentality. He tends to a linguistic monstrosity that rejects normal solutions, underlining a simultaneity that must lead to a very complex spatio-temporal synthesis. In *Annual Rings* (1968), the *assemblage* of places and times which, on the border between Canada and the United States, flowed complementary and parallel, already implied the requirement for surprising perceptive associations. The same could be said of *Arm & Wire* (1968), *Transfer Drawing* (1971) and *Polarities* (1972), where the concatenated projection between metal and flesh, between father and daughter, between magnesium and grass, involves an enrichment due to the combination and integration of signs. Oppenheim tries to establish a real relation, but always invalidates it with precarious combinations that allow him to multiply their expressive possibilities. Thus he couples or intertwines sexually an armchair and a chair in *Two Objects* (1989), he constructs a boxer's gum-shield made of books in *Upper Cut* (1992), he makes an Italian-style divorce dramatic in *Divorce* (1994). Using the relation between things and titles with openly ironic and critical intent, he finds improbable but possible visual and cognitive connections in *Sleeping Dogs* (1997).

His attitude is restless, it does not tranquilize but disturbs with the dialectics of appearances. He apparently chooses banal, mediocre, popular figures such as the boot, the glass, the tea-pot, or well-known representations of human and animal bodies, the dog's head, the dolphin's tail, the fingers of a man or a woman, the face, the lips, or their internal parts, the liver, the heart, the intestine. They all seem to be chosen from an anonymous set of samples that is not special as a result of the typicality of the representations but as a result of the quantity of real and everyday symptoms and clues that suggest other meanings, nearer to obsession and repression. Oppenheim takes them and characterizes them, he personifies them but never goes so far as to give them a conscience. He works on their enigmatic quality, on their transformation into sphinxes: character/objects. He does not take up a position towards them, he neither condemns nor absolves them, he observes them and tries to reveal their anomalous character. First through the change in scale, then through the new erotic-conflictual, amorous-gestural relationship that allows the object to reveal itself as a *monstrum*, a marvel. In order to obtain this surprising effect, the artist does not distort reality very much. He only establishes different relations which redistribute functions and logic, not only of experience and art, from *Kiss* (1991) to *Kick* (1993), and *Revolving Kissing Racks* (1990), where the extreme behaviour of the artistic object, somewhere between Brancusi and Duchamp, ends up by creating an anomalous mixture of derision and decorum, uprooting and cruelty. It is a sort of murder of the dual identity that he projects onto his victims, things or art, ironic and pitiless glances that follow the imagination rather than logic.

In particular, his constructions bring out an oneiric dimension which is controlled and logical, plausible at the level of artistic thought. They are ambivalent, but possible, like the image of the coffee cup, produced by the dissonance of visual atoms, *Image*

Dissonance. Coffee Cup (1989) or *Black Pool* (1990), where the thought and the project of the player become an explicit visual trace.

The artist, therefore, is able to give great intensity to a reality that in itself is insignificant, he passes from objectivity to subjectivity, he produces the pleasures of seeing things and stories tossed about from one situation to another, always with the irony that characterizes, protects and saves him. The ironic force gives a detached progress and calls into question the strong subjective connotation as well as the distressful seriousness: *Aging* (1974) and *Murder in Hawaiian Shirts* (1989).

Elsewhere the dislocation of the use and the function of images that intersect and pierce each other leads to a *unicum* which always plays on two points of view of art, internal and external, personal and impersonal, which in their symmetrical arrangement combine together to assume a series of unstable, ineffable and uncertain meanings: *Second Generation Image. Iron/Boat* (1990). Elsewhere the combination of elements gives physical weight to one language and lightens another. In *Badly Tuned Cow* (1988), the score is concrete while the animal is absorbed in the musical path. Continuous negations and reappropriations that bring Oppenheim's work towards an area of surreal poetry, where the object is captured, decontextualized and metamorphosized, so that it extends into another. This leads to an effect of instability which in some works involves a sexual ambiguity, like in *Toe to Heel. Woman trapped in a Man's Body)* (1990), where the erotic-seductive identities that emerge from objects such as the cowboy boot or the girdle become interchangeable, act on each other, disguise themselves, move around and simulate a continuous passage of the being.

It is on this passage, linked to "bad figures", that the objects, like in Dalí or Breton, make love, *Two Objects* (1989), or applaud,

Slow Clap for Satie (1989), or that the bodies are transformed into tools, *Lungs with Brushes Heart with Paper Liver with Pencil* (1992). As well as being ironic and surprising, the couplings imply a threat of imminent catastrophe. They are moments of death, they suggest a fracture or a limit. At times, in fact, they get lost and end up scattered around, like fragments of a body in the process of decomposition which is spreading around its parts. An exit, therefore, from the utopia of a metaphorical design, capable of integrating and harmonizing all monstrosities for an experience of disorder and loss, with the subsequent uncontrolled convulsion.

At the crossroads of these constructions, signs and symptoms of a subjective, though real vision, is the distancing of art as truth or utopia. Like all good realists and cynics, Oppenheim does not believe in the work of art as example, but as loss, turbid and threatening. He does not intend to establish the topography of a vision, to provide a consolatory order, demarcated by frontiers and places. Coming from the crossing of a unique and absolute knowledge, like that professed by Minimal Art and Conceptual Art, he declares himself to be interested rather in imperfect and chaotic manifestations, in the dispersion and disorder that create confusion and flux, dialogue and tension. He wants to convey his extreme fragility, which in the early years had been linked to the destiny of his body and now is linked to the destiny of his daily life, made up of a casual survival, which can no longer be related to an elective discourse, now abandoned. No more sublime objects, but banal objects that come from the behavioural exploration of society, the experimentation of its uncertainty and wandering, in which the risk of getting lost is another suspense.

Dennis Oppenheim, in the late 1950's

Germano Celant Personally, I think that it is important to understand the roots of an artist from as early as possible. So my first question is about your education as a youth. What kind of books or creative material were around during your adolescence? Were you exposed to art or literature at that time?

Dennis Oppenheim I grew up during the 1940s in a suburban area of California, which was rather conformist. My father was from Russia, born in China and my mother was American. My father was an engineer. My mother was very interested in music, poetry, art and literature. Basically I had a good home for becoming an artist. I developed an interest in making things from a very early age. I acquired many of the personality traits I still have. I find myself capable of being alone. Unknown to me, I was probably displaying the basic characteristics of someone in a creative profession. Sometimes I was withdrawn, although in the community there was a great urge from the outside to conform to your peers, to the conventions that existed during that prelude to the 1950s.

GC Did you do much reading? Go to a library much?

DO I found myself more able to engage in nonacademic activities, visceral ones involving manual dexterity, that kind of thing. I was surrounded by music, mostly classical music. My parents created the atmosphere for academic achievement, although I was not terribly involved in that direction.

GC Was your father's profession as an engineer relevant to your understanding of structure, of the articulation of buildings or geometry?

DO My father tried to teach mathematics to me from age ten on and failed miserably. I realized then that I didn't have the facility for technical achievement and exactitude, that I seem to operate in a "soft zone" of visual art. Failing in the pursuit of mathematics and science, feeling stifled in that area may have broadened my entry into art. I accepted the fact that science was difficult for me and eventually rejected it as a possibility.

GC Did you go to see films? What was the cultural context of Electric City? Did you go to museums?

DO Films were very important to me and still are. I would go to films back in the 1940s with my parents every week. Of course then it was film noir which I found fascinating, probably because I was relating to the structure without knowing what structure was, the way things were put together, the scenes. I think

17

this was one of the most profound early experiences for me outside of visual stimuli from books, illustrations and things. Later on I wondered why I didn't go into film and film production. Electric City did not exist culturally speaking. There were no museums there. I have trouble with museums, especially historical museums. It's an odd thing to say but a museum is not a place I am dying to visit in any city. I guess underneath that difficulty is the realization that my interest in art is an art that is yet to be made.

GC You had some non-art related hobbies as a teenager, including rifle shooting. What does it mean to you now, looking back at it?

DO In suburban California in the late 40s and early 50s, there was tremendous pressure to conform and it's probably true, that I was demonstrating certain conflicting aptitudes. One would think of an aptitude in art as precluding other interests in areas that seem incongruent, but I was very active in sports and other things. Shooting a rifle I enjoyed doing, and racing cars and things of that sort. During the 50s I was operating as a teenager, not really recognizing the inclinations to other things that became very strong later.

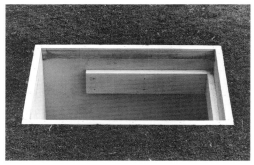

GC What was your high school experience like?

DO Richmond High was in the industrial section of the Richmond El Cerito combine. I lived in El Cerito and I could have gone to a different high school, but my parents chose to send me to an extremely public high school. This was in an industrial city and most of the students came from working class families. There was even a marginally unemployed faction. It was probably one of the lower institutions in California at that time. I'm not exactly sure why, but I look back with pleasure at my experience there. It was typical American Graffiti.

GC As a student, who were your teachers? Were any of them a special influence?

DO Often in high school, the art teacher was splitting his/her time between physical education and art, filling what the school considered relatively unimportant positions.
The assignments in high school were not memorable. But in the lower classes, in elementary school, there were occasions when during an art project I would definitely feel inspired and pulled into some special orbit. I was much more animated and more inclined to engage things than the rest of the students. So there were periods when I would ebb and flow through this matrix of non-professional instruction to find a certain acuity, a certain possession, indicating where my interest would lead later on.

GC What seemed to be the most prominent art movement when you were in high school? Still Abstract Expressionism? What were you looking at?

DO I remember Abstract Expressionism being extraordinarily potent in my mind as an adolescent. A de Kooning was remarkably seductive to me in my late teens. I was particularly drawn to the sheer sort of anti-painting he did, how he

Viewing Station #2, 1967
Photo The New Museum, New York

Excavated Sculpture # 3, 1967
Photo The New Museum, New York

would push the brush across the canvas backward and create this extraordinary visual modulation. Still untrained, unsophisticated, I read a visual phenomenon without even having a vocabulary.

Abstract Expressionism surrounded me during the late 50s, close to when I entered art college, which was 1958.

GC What do you remember of the time you entered art school? What plans for a career did you have?

DO I felt really removed and lost the first year or so, particularly entering an arena as mysterious as art. It was very different in the late 50s from what it is today. Everything was strange, the teaching of art, the students, the teachers. I was looking at it a little bit from the outside. This however changed the second year, but as far as going to artist's studios — one didn't even necessarily talk to a professor after a class.

There weren't many people blessed in the 50s with the kind of acuity and sense of the future that would allow them to know, necessarily, where their aptitudes lay. One had no idea of how to survive anyway, and going to art school was really a way of throwing it to the wind. In 1959, there was not much difference between commercial art and fine art. Perhaps commercial art might have afforded you some ability to make a living, and at that early stage, one was really just testing the waters to see what might develop. However, in my sophomore year, it was clear that I was not interested in commercial art and for me this was a relatively quick awakening.

GC After only two years in art school, you got married and moved to Honolulu. What was this period like?

DO I quit school and went to Hawaii when I married. In 1959 Kristin, my first child was born. I later had two more children, Erik and Chandra, from a second marriage.

So to make a living I did use the abilities I had in commercial art. I look at this period as a kind of hiatus, a period where I temporarily abandoned any serious involvement in art making. Living in Honolulu during the early 60s, I was busy with a family and trying to support myself.

GC You returned to California, studying and teaching in the Bay Area from 1961 to 1965. What was the art scene like there at the time? Who do you remember as influential?

DO I did return to the university after being divorced in Hawaii, and I began to return to art making. This took some doing, but I quickly regained the spirit I had as a sophomore at the California College of Arts and Crafts in 1959. When I returned to finish my junior and senior years, I was older and more comfortable talking to other artists, even semi-well known artists. I would go into San Francisco often and down to Los Angeles occasionally. In other words, I was maturing and developing, looking at a broader spectrum. I was, however, not familiar with the East Coast at that time which seems astonishing. There seemed

19

to be a large art world to grapple with in California; there were things happening in Los Angeles, as well with Kienholz and others.

I was interested in what was referred to as West Coast Neodada. There was a tendency among Bay Area artists toward the term "funk" which was from music, meaning off-key. The Bay Area sensibility was largely given over to this notion of off-key, dissonance, a kind of visual dysfunction, an image of destruction. This interested me immediately because it involved abusing convention and disproving the necessity for a continued conventional operation. This basic sensibility was really what prompted my curiosity. 1967 broke in the early conceptual period. Being uncomfortable with art because of its acceptance of certain norms, was to me at that time a positive catalytic function. Much of what I did was aggressively attacking these conventions. The outcomes weren't always successful, and I think a lot of what happened in the Bay Area under the heading of Neodada or "bad painting" wasn't successful. Often outcomes would wallow in unintelligible, personal iconography.

There were artists in my class who began to have success, John McCracken and others. By around 1964 I was getting an idea about what constitutes a career, what avenues might open up, the competition, and so on. In 1965 I went to Stanford to graduate school. I began my serious and truly professional career. That's where the interest in art theory, philosophy and tremendous attention toward the East Coast and a real competitiveness began.

GC You frequently underline this shift of going to Stanford. Why was it so important? Because of the high level of education? Professionalism? Who was teaching there and what ideas were you exposed to?

DO When I first got there, it seemed like half of our teaching staff was having a mid-life crisis, and the other half was in therapy. There were people like Nathan Olivera, a very solid West Coast figurative painter, and Keith Boyle, who was a self-professed formalist operating in a color field area. Frank Lobdel came across as very authentic—his eyes were locked onto Clifford Styl and he portrayed a tragic artist who needed alcohol to enter into the painter's world. I remember having a critique with Frank. The painting I showed during the critique had a drain, like in a sink, painted into the surface, as if the painting all went inside the drain and disappeared. And he said, "I don't know what I think about ideas." This was a classic revelation of the Bay Area attitude, the dismissal of what could be considered a conceptual orientation, and a continued support of the mystique of painting, of trying to originate images through rigorous painting technique. By and large Stanford, although an extraordinary institution, was not the best art school in the nation. With the staff, you probably would have chosen it if you were interested in figurative painting, which was of no interest to me whatsoever. But you did get a feeling of professionalism through osmosis. The high level would rub off onto the art department even though it was undeserving. I worked every day during my graduate period at Stanford. There was not one day when I did not work in the studio almost all day. I produced a tremendous amount of work and became more and more aware of what was happening in Europe and America. It was an extremely intense, valid period.

GC In 1965 and 1966 most of the information on the West Coast was through *Artforum*. Did you read it? Any other sources of contemporary information?

DO Absolutely true. It's probably no secret that *Artforum* has changed since then, but at that time it was a major conduit of information from the East Coast to the West Coast and the other way as well. I think *Artforum* was based initially in the West Coast, at Palo Alto in fact, where I was living. I read everything I could at that point, and had a great interest in the writings of Barbara Rose and the discourse regarding Minimalism. Smithson, Flavin, and Morris' early writings were extremely interesting to me. Robert Morris was writing occasionally at that time. His early theoretical writing regarding Minimalism in the mid-60s were certainly important for me, and I'm sure for others who eventually led the way into conceptual work in the late 60s. The discussion around Minimalism regarding Frank Stella, what was called "deductive painting" fascinated me. The discourse involving Donald Judd and Carl Andre was also of interest and what I considered to be the prevailing cutting edge in art at that time. In reading this material, I easily began to develop visual constructs and intellectual forays into alternatives. In that the writing was by the artists themselves, it afforded an unusually close examination and empathy that I could use to make a closer analysis.

GC What artists did you meet during your graduate education? Sam Francis? Diebenkorn?

DO The artists to know at that time in the mid-60s in the Bay Area were people like William Wylie, Robert Hudson, and of course Bruce Nauman who was a student as well. I never met the practicing artists like Diebenkorn and the artists centered around the San Francisco Art Institute. I believe Wylie conducted a symposium which was not effective at all. Hudson was equally cryptic in his attempt to engage a critique. I would say most of my interactions with the West Coast sensibility were disappointing. There seemed to be a moratorium on verbal acuity. There was in the air a subliminal belief that verbalizing meant weakening the visual rapport with the work and that it wasn't necessary to articulate work as long as you did it well. This is maybe true; but there was general, massive ineptitude on the part of many artists on the West Coast in terms of discussing their work. One of the most delightful things when I came to New York City was that this was simply not the case. There was heated and often inspired exchange in the late 60s between artists to an extent that I do not think exists today.

GC How did you decide to move to New York? It was a big risk.

DO In 1966, after getting my master's degree from Stanford University in April, I was pretty charged up to go to New York. A lot of this energy was through vicarious reading, although certainly on rare occasions I did speak to artists who'd been to New York. As I look back at this period, I see I had a rather sheltered existence. I was almost twenty seven at the time, and compared to young people today, I had relatively little exposure, certainly none to Europe.

Site # 5, *near Philadelphia, Pennsylvania, 1967*

The Bay Area stronghold was in place. The associations I had were corralled within this Bay Area mindset, which included downplaying verbal interchange and this funky, off-key sensibility which did not show any real intellectual rigor. Minimalism could never have been truly developed there. It was far too theoretical in its make-up. So the urge to go to New York was really pretty strong, and in the summer of 1966 I drove across the United States and landed in New York City in June of that year.

GC From 1966 to 1967 your work shifted from painting to other manifestations. Could you describe the change and why it happened? Was it a coherent shift?

DO The work from 1966 to 1967 after Stanford was more didactic. I did a work called *Untitled Table Piece* incorporating upholstered tables, a lmittle like operating tables with just wooden 2'x4's on top. This was clearly a probe into the sub-structure of Minimalism. I also did a stack of white towels using soft relaxed materials. I made the "spool" series which appeared to be rolls of raw canvas. In a work called *Gifts* I gift wrapped several cubes or boxes and stacked them up, one on top of the other. During the summer of 1967, I made *Tomb Stones*, sixteen fiberglass, illuminated grave markers, installed in a serial manner on the floor, one a little larger than the other... Many of these works dealt with the coming death of Minimalism. 1967 was also the summer of the *Excavated Structures* drawings.
In the beginning I was painting, but the painting soon started to give way to sculpture. The painting operated within the West Coast Neodada vernacular, which was somewhat naive in its format, working to find naive devices which would frustrate the picture, put in a purposely bad element, an element that didn't work. All of this turned out to be a very positive precursor to what happened later. Already I was creating an agenda of attack, trying to frustrate the credibility of work that seemed to know how to operate. However, it still operated within the conventions of painting.
Conceptual art took on the real world, a major leap. A similar agenda applied to the sculpture but more superficially. The sculpture did operate in a terrain that could be said to have conceptual roots, involving the conscious notion of frustrating the work. By injecting off-balance elements, injecting awkward placement into it. But the sculpture, no matter how much critical substance it possessed, was still operating under the conventions of the object.

GC How did you make a living? What was it like when you first got to New York?

DO While at Stanford, during my graduate year, I supported myself partly by entering drawing contests, which often would give awards from $25 to $50, sometimes $100. I would win occasionally, or come in second or something like that —it was almost like the state fair, you know, being able to make a great apple pie. In addition to the contests, I made money by teaching in high school. Of course I had to substitute teach because I couldn't take a full-time position. I obtained a teaching credential, which allowed me to teach in junior high and

high school. I knew that with a master's degree you could apply for college teaching, but this was totally outside my realm of possibility.

Having just been a part of a university system, I didn't feel I could really do anything successful unless I was in a lower level teaching position. So I applied for junior high school teaching and sent out about 200 applications. I received one acceptance, which really wasn't an acceptance. It was a letter requesting an interview, but it seemed concrete. This interview was in Smithtown, Long Island, in New York. So in the summer of 1966, I engaged an interview in Smithtown and got the position, beginning in September teaching junior high school in a mid-Long Island town. I had no idea what lay ahead of me. In the summer of 1966 I got a more immediate position working at Mother Goose Nursery School in Far Rockaway, Queens. I was hired as the art teacher for the summer art program in a Jewish school for young people between ten and sixteen. This was my first experience in New York. Brooklyn seemed to be another planet to me and Far Rockaway was even more distant. Fresh out of graduate school, landing here in this very competitive part of the United States, I took the job very seriously. I had a lot of energy, so I worked on lesson plans and developed what I thought would be outrageous projects for young people to do. For a period of two months I put those students through one outrageous project after the other, including making films and all kinds of things. It was an extraordinary success and became my serious beginning point in this new environment, my stepping stone into the New York art world. Teaching in Smithtown, Long Island, wasn't terribly different from Mother Goose. I made weekly trips into New York City and began to meet the artists, mainly at Max's Kansas City which was at that time the only art-oriented bar in the city. There I met people like Frosty Myers, Robert Smithson, and others. I went there every week for that entire year.

GC What artists did you meet at Max's Kansas City?

DO I recall seeking out Walter de Maria, who I hadn't really talked to since high school, where his brother was a friend of mine. Walter was unusual. I recognized that when I knew him as a teenager, although I did not have sufficient sophistication to equate his eccentric nature with anything particular. He seemed strange. He played drums, ran for office and he stood out considerably. I related to something in him that I just didn't have the vocabulary to describe. Visiting him in New York was quite an intense experience for me because I like his work and did manage to get hold of him even though he was then and still is rather difficult to see. I went with a friend. He showed me his color television set which was very new at the time. He was watching baseball while blurring the image so that the white lines would appear very stark on the screen. This was mystifying to me, both to see a color television set and to see it manipulated. He mentioned that he would stay in the room for days and watch it, feeding even more fire to the mystique. Later, we went for a ride around Manhattan; this was 1967. During this ride with Walter there was intense looking at objects or architecture, especially the industrial structures like towers and antennae. There was definitely a consciousness on his part of the way these could play into art. This was probably the last time I saw him, about thirty years ago. Around the same time there was an article in *Artforum* about how Tony Smith took a similar ride on the Jersey Turnpike, beginning his intense move away from object into place and orientation. Of course I had heard about Michael Heizer and I met him on a few occasions. He was a little younger and extremely intense.

GC What kinds of discussions did you have with other artists? What issues seemed important?

DO I remember taking one of my classes at Smithtown during the winter of 1967, outside. We marched around the football field in a line, inscribing lines into the snow. I was beginning to make headway into what became the Earthwork series I developed that year. I continued to visit New York which was about fifty miles away, every weekend; this would center on Max's Kansas City. I met Carl Andre, although I found it almost impossible to discuss anything with him, it was very difficult to have any exchange. Since then he's become quite personable.

In the summer of 1967, Robert Smithson wrote a piece for *Artforum* called "Towards the Development of an Air Terminal Site." This was an extremely catalytic article for me and I wanted to meet him immediately. But it took many months. I had a strong desire to talk about ideas, so I sent a letter to Smithson and told him I'd like to see him. I went to his studio on a Saturday. It was a really intense experience for me. I'd thought about it for weeks and weeks before I went and showed him some of my work, including *Sitemarkers*, models of the *Viewing Stations*, and some of the models of the *Excavated Sculptures*. Out of this meeting developed a sudden connection with Smithson.

GC Describe your friendship with Smithson. What did you talk about when you were together? What memories do you have of it?

DO Of all the artists I met at that time, Smithson was certainly the most important. He seemed to have all the characteristics of an artist, both the troublesome ones and the more radiant. He was gifted verbally, had an extraordinary ability to penetrate subjects. He was well-read. At the same time, art making was difficult for him, and he exuded that sense of difficulty. You got the sense that his objectives were extremely difficult to achieve, his sights were set very high. In the period of 1967 he carried mystique, as if he were operating in a lofty world of constant distraction, constant questioning of what was happening. But his verbal delivery was not contrived. It showed his interest in performance because he was extremely interested in the persona projected. His words were chosen carefully and he was really not given to light communication. During the winter of 1967 I was immersed in the strong dematerialization of the object. I was doing *Viewing Stations*, which one would stand on to look out at land, and excavated structures. When I finally made contact with Smithson and drove into the city, the whole atmosphere was quite intense. The overwhelming idea we shared was that art really operated outside, in the real world. Minimalism had drawn to a close, reached the zero point, and in doing so had begun to activate preexisting object fragments that were usually useless. Our extension of this meant that the necessity of manually and physically originating the work could be abandoned, replaced with a conceptual leap in which one could claim, one could photograph, one could somehow justify possession— methods of trans-

Site # 8, *Port Jervis, New York, 1967*

fer of things found in the real world. This new perception hovered in the atmosphere of my meeting with Smithson. That he was someone who not only understood these factors but did a lot to originate them was really quite satisfying.

GC How did things crystallize in this new perception? How did this new tendency form?

DO The period in 1967 was unique because I started to have the feeling that some of the work could figure in. So the conversations that I had and the intensity surrounding the occasions, the meetings with artists, the looking at exhibitions, were all flavored with apprehension, this intensity that something was going to happen. This atmosphere generated conceptual art. It wasn't as if rain broke out all over the sky and there was a uniform drenching of ideas, it was odd. In the summer of 1967, one of my major constructs seemed on the face of it rather silly. It was really the summer of the hole in the ground. There was an extraordinary importance placed upon one of the effects of Minimalism. The object was no longer there and in its place was a negative place or space. The idea of the hole in the ground seemed catalytic, certainly in the context that developed Earth Art, Land Art. The idea carried numerous implications. First of all, a hole in the ground was sufficiently ambiguous in that it included the negative space of a hole but also a sense of activation around the periphery, the space around it. The hole in the ground also included a sense of immovability, non-movability. It countered objectness, it countered permanence, it united the thing with the place. This one idea alone seemed to open the doors to an entire field, an entire vocabulary that made up the conceptual art domain. In the summer of 1967 this condition was palpable in the atmosphere, held by a number of artists in their own way. This radical agenda included thinking of an extreme alternative to the traditional system, an idea that had profound effects on how we interpret the gallery museum/system. This radical sense neutralized the effectiveness of other work. Suddenly everything else, including Minimalism, became that which generated the more extreme set of principles which became the foundation of Post-Minimalism.

GC How did you relate to the established movements — Pop Art, Minimalism?

DO Under the spell of the summer of the hole in the ground, this radical departure referenced Pop Art and Minimalism in such a way that it set them aside. No matter what one felt about Pop Art in the earlier years — its radical nature, its strong position, its credibility — basically it was painting, and painting was one of the first things that was attacked in this new operation. Claes Oldenburg loomed as a major artist. Oldenburg still figured in certain ways but the agenda that made up the conceptual movement was far different. Early conceptual work was radical, certainly, and it targeted what was immediately around it; Minimalism, Pop Art, other idioms. In the same way that Pop Art trampled on Abstract Expressionism, this work was hopefully destroying the credibility of work that came before it. While this was not necessarily true in the long run, I think it was symptomatic of the overzealous, exaggerated feeling about the level of radicality we felt in the early days.

GC Did you have any contact yet with Europe at this point? With European artists? Critics?

DO In 1967, Europe was beginning to figure in. Beuys' work was beginning to appear in conversations and articles. *Arte Povera* was just beginning to surface. I had inklings of the work of Merz, Kounellis and others. But since the strong focus at this time was the hole in the ground, which enlarged quickly from a hole to a treatment, an activation of outside space, this seemed far more radical than anything that was happening in Europe. The work Beuys and the Italians were doing seemed to be more closely tied to convention. Most of the work was studio-based, gallery-based. It did involve distribution of materials, poured materials, and Beuys' work involved action, a prelude to performance art. But Land Art seemed to be more radical in that it was operating outside this context and more importantly, it was integrating into systems. At that time I was beginning to see a kind of systems art, art that was greatly detached from the traditional format and operating within a new kind of external dynamic.

GC What difference do you see between your early conceptual art and the tradition from the early 60s, from Manzoni to Klein, from Beuys to Fluxus, those who were conscious about the gap between the two universes? Could you elaborate?

DO There is a difference between the mindset of artists like Manzoni, Klein and even Beuys, in comparison to 1967 and 1968 with the conceptual intervention. At least one facet of the difference is that early conceptual art had a strong dialogue with the real world. It did not necessarily always look back over its shoulder and reference atmosphere it was breathing in relation to past art history. There was some of that, but part of the difference was that those artists were far more conscious of their operation within an art world/art historical *continuum*. Klein and Manzoni were operating under a Dada sensibility, and Beuys was operating in the beginning under a quasi-Fluxus sensibility. Even though Minimalism was heavy on our shoulders as we entered into this new arena as soon as the doors opened, it fell in the ground. Land Art was in some important ways distinct from the other conceptual motivations. It operated far more within the physical world than language-based art. It was far more ambitious in some ways than *Arte Povera*, which did not slacken its claims on the requirement for art to bring in a mediated and precious manipulation of materials.

GC Did you have any specific theories in mind? What kind of philosophical texts were you reading?

DO Generally, reading for me was problematic. When I was in a highly productive mode, reading was too much stimulus. However, it's not that I didn't read anything. During this period, 1967-68, I was very interested in Gestalt psychology, phenomenology, scientific texts, and ecology. I was interested in Structuralism, and I read De Saussure on linguistics, things of that sort. I wasn't exactly magnetically pulled toward this material but semiotics were being discussed and I was interested in the conversation. On the whole, if I were to analyze my initial entry into particular artworks, I don't find the inspiration coming from literary or philosophical sources. Perhaps some of this material does sort of coagulate and occasionally swarm silently and invisibly within a secret matrix that is informing my motions but I'm not aware of doing "good art" as a result of extensive intellectual study, of getting information that way. Poetry is certainly more catalytic in its usefulness as a prelude to making art. I was reading Wallace Stevens, Rilke, and Rimbaud. I was very sensitive to the structure of writing. Probably the most interesting work I was reading at that time was between James Joyce and Samuel Beckett. Beckett was extraordinarily potent in terms of the revelation of structure that he was able to bring forth that seemed to operate underneath the page, underneath the words, a consciousness of this secondary language that was operating between the words. This was an example of writing that would overcharge me, and reading three or four pages of *The Unnameable* would send me into some sort of state where I would have to work.

GC Did you find any inspiration in filmmakers like Godard, Fellini, Antonioni, or American film?

DO Film was always important to me from childhood. Going to foreign films was considered necessary in the early 60s and it continued. Godard and Antonioni were interesting to me, although Fellini less so. The structure of these films attracted me again. It was often more interesting than content. Often the content was relatively superficial. In Antonioni's *Zabriskie Point*, the sets and scenes are initiated pretty perfunctorily to set up occasions for the camera to operate in this extraordinarily inspired way. The dialogue was simply thrown in to make figures talk — he was operating on some meta-level of cinematic communication. The interesting thing about Hollywood film is that it establishes an appetite for easily digestible images and sequences. You often go to the film tired, wanting to be entertained, so that a large percentage of films are satisfying on this reduced level, of just absorbing material that is not layered with the demand to rise above it and analyze it. Commercial films provided a major contrast to the job of the fine artist, which was more demanding. There was this feeling that fine art attacks and scrutinizes the world much more severely, so you would walk around with this notion of transcendental hierarchy, where everything was on television and most of what you saw in movies was far beneath the range of the prevailing conceptual art idiom.

GC Did you see Warhol's films? What did you think of them?

DO Warhol's films are a transcendental structural notion placed on top of the medium. Warhol's films are probably, to me, his most influential work. It's odd that this influential work is material that most of us can't look at for more than half an hour. The idea of the catatonic camera was influential in its denial of the conventional formats of film. The catatonic camera created a sort of clinical atmosphere where the subjects were so concentrated on that idiosyncratic overtones would develop. This was a real foray into a scrutiny of a kind of meta-structure that existed underneath things; was communicated through Warhol probably unbeknownst to him.

GC 1967 was a very important year for politics. Were you involved in the anti-war movement or other political struggles? Did your theories engage politics at all?

DO It's odd that I did not engage in any political functions or activities during my entire period at Stanford and before, which included 1964 in Berkeley. I was in Berkeley in 1964 on the sidelines watching the political activity from coffee shops on Telegraph Avenue, never participating. In viewing the marches on Telegraph Avenue, I had a great deal of sympathy and rapport for the movement, but yet there wasn't an initial spark that threw me into it. All I can say is that my main attention during that period and through to 1967 was the satisfaction of operating in a creative intellectual area intensely. The Vietnam War was a kind of exterior, radiant temperature zone that hovered everywhere. It saturated the world every day, every night, it tempered the time. It was as if I was submerged in a membrane and all this external activity was effecting, contrasting and commenting on the superstructure I was engaged in, but I didn't break out of it and enter into the political world. As I recall, the summer of 1967 was the Summer of Love in San Francisco. I went there, not necessarily to engage in the Summer of Love, but in Oakland I did a piece called *Oakland Wedge* which was a geometric cut or slice in a hill. This was definitely my first practiced attempt to make a concrete statement within this new field.

GC Why did you leave the studio to work in the land? Why did you return to California to do *Oakland Wedge*? Was it not possible to do it in New York?

DO I had a trip to make to California anyway, but it's important to realize that *Oakland Wedge* was actually done in the backyard of my parents' home, so it was a little bit like a young person experimenting in the basement. It was really just a test, it wasn't really a significant work. But so much of what came before was theoretical and now there was a hole in the ground, and this was the summer of the hole in the ground.

GC How do you perceive this work from today's perspective?

DO It marked the beginning stages of my moving from oblivion into what could be called visibility. Doing *Oakland Wedge* seemed to be a harmless kind of activity in the backyard of my parents' home, but it is an early example of this atmosphere in which I seemed to be in possession of something. This was one of the first manifestations within an arena that I sensed would generate substance. I never considered this work more than a way to "smell the atmosphere of the soil" to get a feeling of where all this theoretical stuff was going. In many ways, these episodes often become the most real, they're the most un-manipulated, the most shielded from any kind of strategic overtones.

GC Also in 1967, you made a piece called *Sitemarkers*. What was this about? How did it relate to the new ideas you were exploring?

DO Remember, this is the summer of the hole in the ground. It was also in a way the summer of deconstruction, and although we didn't use that word, we were basically deconstructing Minimalism. I wanted to test the notion of whether an existing fragment of an architectural nature in the world could be brought in, successfully possessed by the artist and offered as a credible artwork. With the notion of the found object, the necessity for manual credibility in making the work was no longer an issue, how well could this hold up? In the Sitemarkers, I focused on exterior objects, preexisting fragments of architecture almost like a readymade and considered them to be in my possession through the intervention of photography, with the document able to be exchanged, to be sold. So this sitemarker idea set the foundation for an alternative to object making. I claimed numerous sites during that period, and spent a lot of time driving around. Most of the things that interested me were ground-based, were level with the ground, or were penetrating it. So already I had this sensitivity toward the ground plane. Things that penetrated the ground confused the object-nature of the work. Something that broke the ground would again activate the periphery. There was always ambiguity about the length or the size of the work — where did it start? when did it stop? I was excited about the fact that doors were open on the object and the object was entering into a field, a field of unspecified spatial definition. All of a sudden this notion of a sculpture as place was manifest. Sculpture could not only be placed, but it could be several places, in various locations.

GC How did the experience of *Oakland Wedge* and the *Sitemarkers* change your perception of art? How important was the idea of the "cut" as an intellectual and philosophical gesture to you, in activating the material?

DO I think it's really important to put as much stress as possible on the negative sculptural act because that is really what was behind the initial momentum in 1967-68. We can't forget the importance of Carl Andre in focusing on this ground-based, horizontal condition. The idea of a "cut" was certainly much more rigorously and physically carried out by Heizer. The summer of the hole in the ground was far more catalytic for Heizer than it was for Smithson. The physical subtraction of material from a ground plane is more conventional if one thinks about it related to the traditional subtractive method of sculpture. The more cerebral direction taken by Smithson and others can be seen as more challenging than the continuation of the conventions of traditional sculpture. Trying to implement visionary new ideas can be tricky, however. Allan Kaprow and his entry into Happenings, for example, was an extraordinarily visionary idea that may have failed because not enough critical decisions were made. It was given too much latitude to slide between sculpture and theater so that it became in some ways unintelligible. With this new direction in my work, I was conscious of the fact that if you let the doors open too wide, and relinquish entirely the contact with traditional sculpture, you're going to lose it. You're going to lose yourself in the sheer immensity of the system that is going to engulf and finally render unintelligible the artistic intervention. In a phase like this, where everything seems to be opening up, coming into possession in a new, exciting way, it's easy to become intoxicated by the sheer fantasy of moving from oblivion to visibility. You begin to feel you've invented new concepts, that you own them.

Sitemarker #6, Northport, Long Island, 1967

Your artistic persona can lead you to believe that you really did originate these ideas, which is often simply not true. No one invented a "cut" and no one invented a hole in the ground. These ideas were brought forth subliminally and through osmosis in various ways, so we were playing out our own nuances, based on a certain shared philosophical foundation.

GC Let's talk about *Annual Rings*, 1968, the famous piece about physical contact. What did this intersection of lines and boundaries mean to you?

DO We're in 1968, we're in the fire now. Everyone is scrambling to claim as much territory as possible. Cameras are clicking, people are scurrying around, again trying to stake their claim. The doors are open. The cat's out of the bag. I was looking at ecological textbooks. If I were to venture out into the terrain, which in many ways I saw as like the surface of a painting, if I were to engage in this new terrain abstract gesture, I did not want to be dependent upon traditional iconography, traditional image making. So I decided that I should make lines on these flat planes, but reference information so that the lines would mean something besides their formalist selves. So in *Annual Rings* I took schemata of tree rings and reproduced it on the boundary between Canada and the United States. The boundary line would run between, pierce, go through the middle of the tree rings. What made this piece interesting to me was that it was located on a boundary. The idea of operating on a political boundary was really foreign to our sculptural heritage and opened what became the concept of "site-specific" sculpture. The term actually developed a bit later, in the context of artists like Mary Miss, Scott Burton, Siah Armajani and others, where there was a perceived need to legitimately site works so they had an integral connection to the site. It was a kind of Zen relationship. They wanted the work to be in harmony with the site.

This was not at all true in the early 1968 period. It was more of a vicious, almost aggressive intervention. It was more of a disruption of the site. This work did not want to refer to the picturesque and to the sublime, it wanted to deal with the rigor of the site as it was a condition of the real world. This is where the site works of 1968 and the legitimacy of their occupation of the physical zone was peppered by the real-time and the political atmosphere of that period. That's where the energy of something like the Vietnam War could subliminally get into the blood track of the work, and stimulate it into a condition that would not necessarily be easily replicated during a period of more mediated distance. It was clear that once the doors were open, you didn't want to find yourself sitting on a hillside looking at a sunset.

GC In the radical shift to move into the land in 1967, it seems as though you were abandoning all the traditional tools of the artist. There seems to be a new use of dependence on photography in particular. Could you comment on this?

DO With this opening of the doors around 1967, in one fell swoop we confronted almost all the issues that were part of traditional art. Much of this centered on the dematerialized object, the fact that the object no longer had to be rigid, no longer had to be possessed directly, no longer even had to be seen directly.

Annual Rings, *USA/Canada boundary at Fort Kent, Maine and Clair, New Brunswick, 1968*

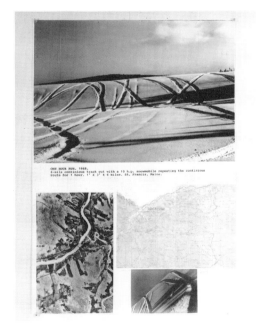

Information about the work could be convincingly generated via the photograph. At the time, we entered into the credibility of the photograph naively, as a byproduct of the focus on these dematerialized conditions. It was later that it became such a central and influential force in its own right. The only conscious thought about extending this work via photography at the time was that professional photography was not interesting, so the relationship to the history of photography was played down. The conscious desire was to have this method of documentation seem matter-of-fact, to seem almost purposely mediocre so that the focus wouldn't necessarily be on the photograph as an object of art, but as a vehicle for the larger concept. The documentation was a kind of photographic residue of the piece. It was only with the second generation conceptual artists, basically the Metro Pictures group, that the photograph itself became the central issue — this concern was relatively secondary in the so-called classical period of conceptualism.

There's been a lot said about the unsuccessful use of photography as a medium to communicate this radical work, but I find it more an indication of where the energy was. The energy was in the work. Operating alone in a field you knew that this information was going to be handed out second-hand through texts and photography. I remember being at the Earth Art show at Cornell, curated by Willoughby Sharp, and driving around with the students, including Gordon Matta-Clark, looking for possible sites to do work. At every turn the car seemed to bring into focus a land mass or a location that could be transformed into an art work. I kept jumping out of the car and doing things on the land quickly, photographing them. The students wondered how I could live in this world, seeing everything as a place for possible intervention. This period didn't last very long, but it is an indicator of the absolute openness of this new situation. It wasn't just about intervening, it was also about the fact that this information could be transferred photographically, that with a text opposite it becomes intelligible, concrete, and interesting.

GC What is the relationship of time to your work? Were you interested in making physical gestures, or did you think about more abstract concepts like time?

DO The assertion of time is always abstract at best. The interesting question here is the function of a performance-related form within the Earthwork vernacular. I was definitely not interested in bringing in performance as an element because of the way it related to the theatrical ambiguity of Happenings, and I didn't want Earthworks to be necessarily related to that. For its own safety, I wanted it to relate most directly to formalist sculpture, although I was very sure it had to transcend that as well. Works that had to be recorded sequentially through photographs, such as *One Hour Run* or *Time Line*, had a sensitivity to time, but I see these works as concrete because they were grounded in a sculptural precedent, which provided the most profound leap. If Land Art primarily referenced performance, it wouldn't have had nearly the impact that it did. It was because it was related to objects and the transcendence of the tradition of object making that it had its most profound impact.

GC What was the impact of the "Earthworks" show curated by Robert Smithson at the Dwan Gallery in 1968? What was the climate for Conceptual Art? How did your participation in the show affect you?

DO The "Earthworks" show at Dwan Gallery in 1968 was extremely important. The summer preceding it, I did a large model of a piece called *Mount Copaxi Transplant*. I wanted to suggest the scope that opened up in the summer of 1968. I made a model of a very large idea that I wasn't in a position to execute, which made it largely conceptual. I located the geographic center of the United States in Lebanon, Kansas, which is all wheat fields. I took a schemata of concentric rings from Mount Copaxi in South America, which I would plow into this wheat field. It was site-specific in the sense that the apex, the center of the volcano registered as a circular line cut into the crop was to coincide exactly with the geodesic center of the United States.

The "Earthworks" show, which included Heizer, de Maria, Morris, Andre and others, is really magnified in my memory. It seemed like everything floated down into this exhibition like particles from outer space. It was there that I learned about the competitive, political strata and the atmosphere surrounding the art world, all in one experience. My role in that show was relatively minimal. I showed the model and I think I put up a snapshot, a small one, of something I'd done in a wheat field. Since I had no experience of being in an important exhibition, I came across as somebody who had thrown things together that were not terribly physically impressive. I did feel that I needed to somehow devalue the credibility of a gallery show, that this work was fugitive to it. Attempts to show the work had to be frustrated. In a sense, I wanted to turn into a kamikaze and destroy my own credibility.

By contrast, the exhibition seemed to be very gallery-oriented. It was not at all necessarily disruptive. In the show was a giant transparency of Heizer's *Double Negative* which was certainly an astonishing work. Everybody was extremely impressed by the fact that he had pulled this off during the summer, definitely a tour-de-force. Walter de Maria showed a large painting with a plaque on it that said something like "the color men choose to attack the earth" — I thought the exhibition was going to present all the discoveries of the past year, all the open doors in to the land. All of a sudden there was Dada work by De Maria that seemed to negate everything that Smithson was interested in. There was a work by Robert Morris that was basically a physical activity: a lot of loose materials thrown onto the floor including earth and maybe coal and grease and felt and other things, which in the end seemed also to be countering, trying to sabotage what appeared to be a clean urge to deal with outside systems.

GC You first travelled to Europe in 1969. What was your first contact, what was this experience like?

DO By that time I already had my first exhibition at John Gibson's of Earthwork models. There was already a great deal of press surrounding conceptual art and particularly Land Art. It was reviewed in *Time, Life*, and *Newsweek*, and of course all the art magazines, so the work was beginning to become quite well-known. My first show in Europe was at Yvon Lambert in Paris, and he showed photo documentation. That summer I also made a trip to Stedelijk Museum to

Time Line, USA/ Canada time boundary at Fort Kent, Maine and Clair, New Brunswick, 1968

Mount Copaxi Transplant, 1968 Collection of the Metropolitan Museum of Art, New York

see the early conceptual art shows done by Willem van Beeren This was my entry into the European arena. It was very engaging. I began to feel connectedness with other artists and to see the effectiveness of my work in relationship to other young artists. Since I had such ambitious plans regarding Land Art, I tended to see museum shows as being a throwback to a more traditional idiom. I wanted my work to exist outside museum shows. For the Stedelijk Museum I contacted a farm in Holland and did a very large work called *Cancelled Crop*. Of course it didn't play much in terms of the exhibition, it was only included with the photograph. But I did feel at the time that somehow I was not easily usurped into the exhibition format.

GC What kind of connections did you sense with Italian and French artists?

DO Initially there was not much affinity between Land Art and what was going on in Italy and France. As the work became more refined and developed offshoots like Body Art and Process Art, there developed more of a rapport with the Italians at least. Certainly artists like Kounellis, Merz and others. Zorio, Penone, and Pisani were interesting ; however, they were all engaged in a certain finessing of the materials that one didn't find in the American work, certainly not in Land Art. The Italian body-related works always seemed to have an element of historical reference, posturing, adornment, masquerade, things that were certainly interesting but definitely not real-time severed nerves that existed in the American work.

GC How did Land Art evolve into Body Art? What was the transition like?

Installation, Yvon Lambert, Paris, 1969
Photo André Morain

Cancelled Crop, *Finisterwolde, Holland,*
1969

DO I always say that when I was walking around on the land, I suddenly became aware of my body. I'm not sure how true this is. Land Art seemed to be silently and secretively taking over my body, a bit like the *Body Snatchers*. The body loomed as a vital area of fertile possibility, and it was easy for me to give in to it. Land Art transcended traditional sculpture, using ephemeral materials, dematerializing itself. Later as film and time sequences emerged, when the work was beginning to employ performance, there was a very natural transition to the body. There was an urge to create a crossover, a point where the immersion in these large-scale projects could give way to an entry into another world of physical self-absorption. The early Body Art films didn't employ great virtuosity in terms of film work. It's interesting to think how these films might be related to Warhol's catatonic camera. Usually the camera was put on a tripod and pointed at the direction of the activity. The camera was on for thirty minutes, so the outcome was very clinical. There was no interest in making it interesting outside of the objective merits of the piece. In a way, this work was influenced by the Warholian aesthetic. That may be a weakness or a strength. While it did not necessarily come from Warhol, the method of photographing it seemed to consciously use his sterile, unmanipulative method of recording as a way of showing the material.

GC Were you influenced by contemporary dance or music performance? I'm thinking of people like Trisha Brown, Lucinda Child, Philip Glass, Steve Reich, etc.

DO Performers were only peripherally interesting to me. Body Art wasn't about theater or classical performance. Almost all the videotape and the documentation projects were done in seclusion, without an audience, in real time, with very little attention given to theatrical structuring. It was an attempt to capture a clinical, almost scientific observation of events as they unfold, fracture, fade out and exhaust. Fundamentally it was about extending the sculptural domain. I wanted to maintain alignment with the traditional use of inert materials in the process of sculpture making.

GC In both Land and Body Art there seemed to be an idea of transit or transaction between two territories. Did they share the same vision, to change or intensify a "surface" as almost any artist does? How did this relate to traditional painting?

DO The repercussions of the hole in the ground were far more extensive than the simple act. As Land Art developed, it developed a critical position. It depended on the use of photography. I did see much of this work as referencing painting — when I looked at a photograph of an Earthwork I tended to associate the linearity with painting, with drawing. But the core idea was still its dematerialization of the object, connecting it to traditional sculpture, that was its substance. As the work became transformed into Body Art, the body-related work demanded the same careful treatment, but with a link to traditional painting. So you had the cut, the scratch, the exploration of skin and body surface in almost the same way you would see an operation on canvas.

Reading Position for Second Degree Burn, in which my chest, partially shielded by a book, was sunburned, was closely related to the idea of painting. I wanted to reference painting, but to extend it, to see how to move ahead of it. In comparison to painting, Body Art was an extremely economical method of art making. There were no tools. There was no extraneous material. The action and the surface acted upon were united in the same system. The works were both subject and object, both the tool and the victim, the initiator and the recipient. This was an extremely dense configuration in which to operate. It was one of the most radical formats in the spectrum of conceptual art, it was certainly more visceral than language-based work. The body as surface was almost like a painting with feeling. It was as if the material finally came alive. As the body was attacked, put into states of exhaustion, states of danger, these acts were registered within the sensory system. When the body was violated, there were often very clear visual repercussions, but it was clear that it was operating on a higher sensory level.

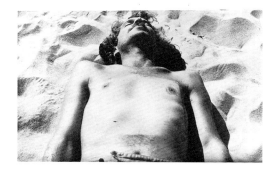

GC Tell me more about the various manipulations of the body in this work, about the sensory elements.

DO There were certain obvious aspects of body material. Some things you could detach from the body like hair or fingernails. There were obvious limitations in terms of method of performance. You could create too much sensory stimulus for the viewer. If it went too far into what appeared to be a possible mutilation, it would read in a negative way. Like Land Art, Body Art came from the real

Film Installation, Gingerbread Man, *Yvon Lambert, Paris, 1971*

Reading Position for Second Degree Burn, *Jones Beach, New York, 1970*

world, operated in the real world, did not want to associate with theater, did not want to associate with artifice. It didn't necessarily need an audience. It emerged from an art that made it possible to do things at home, with nobody looking, and using the camera as a recording device. In many ways, the legitimacy of documentation and the credibility of photographic information brought about by Land Art allowed Body Art to materialize.

GC How did you relate to the sexual connotations of the body? So much of it is about penetration, transfer, and so that it seems natural to read sexual metaphor in it.

DO My early Body Art played down sexual content. Works like *Vertical Penetration*, where I slid down an embankment or dove into the water pretending to be a knife may have appeared to have sexual content. Really there was a conscious effort on my part to sidestep it. These works addressed more traditional sculptural acts found in art making, a process. A few works brought in the sexual element in a conscious way. I stayed away from this content because I didn't feel comfortable with it. I didn't feel as if I could operate successfully with that content. Others certainly pursued it, but for me it simply did not seem to be the time to address it. I had this strong feeling it just wasn't right for me.

GC The period in which you engaged most of your Body Art work was relatively brief. Why did you abandon the format so quickly?

DO Body Art moved very quickly. From the inspiration of using the body as a sort of canvas it wasn't long before it entered into an exploration of psychological states. After a year or so, I was doing collaborative works with my children. I engaged questions about time, longevity, genetics, working through an agent to get access to areas that aren't possible to get to because of lifespan. Things of this sort became the content of the work. Body Art as an occupation had a relatively short life. If you think about Land Art, most of the important works were done in three or four years, but still some artists have been working in it for decades because it has such a rich horizon. Body Art probably didn't. It seemed to be an art that was burning itself up. Since Body Art was not about virtuosity or developing a theatrical persona, original Body Art demanded to be transcended the next day, to be quickly extrapolated from and moved beyond. It was a fast search and it burned its bridges.

GC Tell me about *Polarities*, 1972. How do you see this work relating to Body Art?

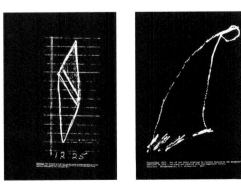

Preliminary test for Vertical Penetration, *near Boise, Idaho, 1970*

Polarities, *1972*

DO *Polarities*, 1972 seems to me to be a relatively successful work that invoked elements of both Land and Body Art. My father had recently died. I found a drawing on his desk, presumably one of the last diagrams that he drew. It was just an unconscious diagram that he probably did while he was on the telephone. My daughter was about a year old. I found one of her first recognizably anthropomorphic drawings, that definitely looked like a figure. I enlarged and juxtaposed both of them and plotted them on a field with magnesium flares, which I

35

photographed from the air while the magnesium burned at night. I was using a lot of ephemeral material at the time. In 1972 I also did *Shadow Projection* which was really a memorial for my father. It was the projection of a 2,000 foot negative band of shadow down a carbon arc light. I showed both works together using a slide-dissolve system. Polarities prefaced a series of works that I did with my children, which represented a cooling down from the hot Body Art of 1970 into the surrogate performers in 1974. In one piece with my son, I drew on his back as he simultaneously tried to reproduce the same drawing on the wall. I always considered those works to be about longevity and how to operate as an artist after death. It was interesting to think of my children as being capable of carrying, genetically, certain impulses past the point that I could. Conceptually, it wasn't enough just to operate within the domain of your lifetime. Given the license made available through the believability of conceptual information, one could speculate on an art that could be enacted by someone else after the point you departed. These initial works with my children function within that arena of genetic extension.

GC Tell me more about the shift into "surrogate performers." What was the significance of this shift? Why this step away from your own body?

DO Body Art as I practiced it from 1971 to 1973 was always complemented with other works, installations, things of this sort. In 1974 Body Art moved into installations. It was time to move on. Marionettes I was familiar with because I made them as a child. They seemed to be an obvious way of continuing the performance-related self-referential autobiographical work without being physically part of the engagement. I developed surrogates, as I called them, which were 18-inch high marionettes — some of them danced from mechanically driven strings and others talked with a mechanical voice-activated lower jaw, like Charlie McCarthy. These moving marionettes were first used in a piece called *Theme for a Major Hit* in which they performed a song that I wrote, with the lyrics "it ain't what you make, it's what makes you do it." In 1974, art was deeply involved in interrogating itself. *Theme for a Major Hit*, using lyrics, pointed out the necessity to pin down the motive for making art. It was simply that virtuous expression of art energy is not as important as why you're doing it. Often artists are making art because they want to make money, they want to become famous, for all kinds of reasons. When you look at the work, it's somehow weakened because the agenda was subliminally something else.

GC How is your work today affected by, informed by your Body Art work?

DO There's an article by Stuart Morgan called "Gut Reaction" in which he discusses the stomach as a region that is important in the art making process. I would quite agree. I am very familiar with states of actual decision making that couple with the intellectual element in this sort of mid-body feeling, intuition. One of the works to be exhibited in Venice is called Heart with Paper. Liver with Pencils. Lungs with Brushes. There are three organs, a heart, a lung and a liver, very large, made of hard foam covered with a combination of broken black glass and black resin. Each organ contains some art material. The heart has rolled

Polarities, *Bridgehampton, New York, 1972*

Shadow Projection, *Batavia, New York, 1972*

paper coming out of its ventricles, the lung has brushes coming out of one of its portholes, and the liver has a fistful of pencils protruding from one of its lobes. They are all spinning, turning slowly from a ceiling motor. This work was shown about four years ago and it has always been an important work to me because it's about the non-cerebral sources for making art. This piece has in common with Body Art the interest in interrogating the art making process as it intersects the body, on a deep, internal level.

I found certain things just captivating within the range of Body Art. Sweating, for instance. The body exudes it due to overexertion, as sweat gets into your eyes it blurs your vision, and as you shake your head rapidly, the sweat starts to spring off and hit something or fall on something. So the body is producing this blurred vision, residue, enveloped in heat and vapor. All of these things can be played into an expressive scenario with the temperature, with rhythm. While this was examined back in the 70s, these things still creep into the recent work. There are definite connections. A piece I did a few years ago called *Galloping through the Wheat* had bronze horses descending from the air onto a loaf of bread (actually made of foam), slicing through it and continuing through the wall. This kind of cutting device, these raging stallions bisecting the soft material very much relates to the early work. The interest is in passage from one place to another or severing parts from the whole.

GC From time to time, your work has used animals — like dogs, insects, etc. — for its completion. It appears that this animal iconography has returned again in recent works of the 80s-90s, as you've just mentioned with *Galloping through the Wheat*. Are these manifestations related?

DO During the early 70s I did a number of works using outside agents. I did a piece called *Material Interchange* where I used a mosquito that bit me, extracted blood and then became airborne. I considered this material displacement, putting myself in aerial suspension. Again, this refers to separating (blood from the body), the desire to relocate, distribute, dislocate elements of yourself. I did another piece called *Protection* where I designated a rectilinear area with hired attack dogs that guarded it, thus creating an inaccessible space - very precious because of that. It was a way of commenting on the phenomenon of how guards standing next to art works in a museum seem to make the work more important. Within the new sculptural vernacular of the recent work, I continue to use animal imagery. They often seem to be the agent necessary to push through an idea.

GC The instability of certain materials seems quite important in your work from the 70s to today. What sort of energy does it represent to you? How does it function?

DO In 1969 I did *Infected Zone* in Milan. I was interested in the difference between infection and sterilization, dirty and clean. I was interested in the fact that you could clean something and it wouldn't look much different. The idea came from doing works on polluted ground and showing a contrast between the pastoral, the tranquil world and the real world. I burned the grass and set traps.

Theme for a Major Hit, *1974*

In the gallery I cleaned the floor and put down rat poison, so there was this contrast of material. The rat poison was a granular powder, so you could see it as the alternative form of a solid. It's important to stress the use of unstable materials in Process Art and early conceptual art and installations. This was a major component of the recipe. I did a number of *Gallery Decompositions*, where the materials in the gallery were broken down into their unstable forms, powder. I would have a pile of material on the floor and the title would say "the material is a place on which it rests without the catalyst." This was a type of pseudo-chemistry. I would make a pile of sawdust and claim that it was the floor dematerialized. It was a place without the architectural catalyst that made it rigid.

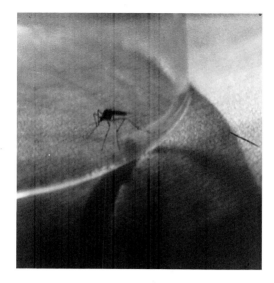

GC In some ways related to this instability principle is the element of fire, which appears often in your work. What is its function, for instance, in a work like *Digestion. Gypsum Gypsies* of 1988-89?

DO *Digestion. Gypsum Gypsies* is comprised of a group of fiberglass deer with antlers that have plumbing to allow gas jets to emit flames from the antlers. A few of the deer are cut in half and positioned as if they're emerging from the wall. The piece basically turns the deer into furnaces, they're burning themselves up. In doing so they're digesting the room, the gypsum that covers the walls. They continue to burn up and render in this burning flame a new material state of the gallery. I've done a number of other works with fire over the years. In the early 80s I did fireworks pieces that used an architectural, sculptural complex as an armature. In some cases these giant works referred to Russian Constructivist sculpture, except the architectural element was given a secondary function, as the framework for rockets that would leave traces, like lines. They were almost drawing machines. Again, it was a manifestation of the desire to get away from the object by making it subservient to another function. Looking back, it was a way to get back into structure, after doing work on film and video. I wanted to get back to the issues generated ten years earlier, the idea of horizontal ground-based sculpture as place, the hole in the ground, the energy field, the installation issues. They had fallen into a temperate zone that was at rest, and I had the choice of stirring them back up or moving on.

GC In the mid-70s how was the art scene changing? What was your relationship at that time to the European artists?

Material Interchange, *1970*

Protection, *1971*

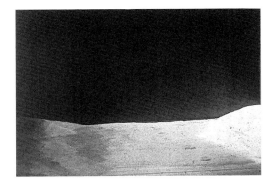

Detail of Infected Zone, *Milano, 1971*

Gallery Decomposition, *1968*

DO I will always associate artists like Kounellis, Merz and Beuys with this period of my development, when I surfaced on the art scene. While they started to exhibit in New York in the early 70s, there was still significant resistance to European artists here, especially when you compare it with the number of Americans exhibiting in Europe. I was familiar with them mostly through the magazines because the occasions to see their work in person were relatively rare. I didn't often see an actual Merz. Kounellis was quite rare, although I did see one of his performances. He was always very interesting to me. Beuys I met a number of times — I was around when he did I love America and America loves me and I went to see him when he was at Rene Block. Needless to say, I found him quite extraordinary.

GC At the end of the 70s you began to add light and sound. What is the significance of sound in your work? Is it a different energy or material? How does it relate to your recent work?

DO When I get excited about an idea for a work, I feel it rushing into the cold air where I can grab it, compare it, figure out how it holds up. I never feel that intensely about the genesis of a monologue or a sound piece. I've never been totally possessed by the function of sound in a work to the degree of originating an idea. I've done a number of pieces with drums, which are hard to make a mistake on. The equivalent in sculpture is the use of rocks. It's very hard to see a rock you don't like. Music is a whole other thing. When I bring it into the work, I never feel fully in possession of it. If I really could possess it, I'd be a musician.

GC Toward the end of the 70s you did a number of pieces that emphasized machinery, a mechanical aspect. Is this a meta-image of art for you, the idea of a work that is made to manufacture the art experience?

DO The period from 1975 to 1977 was troubled. I was doing installations that were progressing with difficulty. The early machine pieces came around 1978, including *Falling Room* and *Exit for the South Bronx*. I had a strenuous agenda of wanting the art to interrogate, to use art to diagnose what was happening. In 1978-79 I did a piece in Seattle called *Waiting for the Midnight Special. (A Thought Collision Factory for Ghost Ships)*, which was comprised of many mechanical components. A giant circular depressed disk with a railroad track turned, to address certain quadrants. One of the quadrants was a smokestack and incinerator. Another was a tunnel that would slowly cover itself as it approached the depot. There was a vent that went out to the ocean and then a system of molds and templates. I thought of this as a kind of factory that could do a number of things. You could visualize energy moving into the tunnel and by engaging the switch track you could direct it toward a combustion chamber, towards a template, or towards a series of molds where impressions could be made. I thought of this depot as an exteriorization of my mind, and in projecting it outward it became like a catcher's mitt, something broad that could catch things. It was as if part of my mind had been replicated using these architectural, industrial counterparts. They were waiting for the entry of an idea force, that would then be thrown around in various conduits. This is the beginning of a kind of structural thinking as I saw it. I was turning these large structural factories into metaphors for thought processes. This closely related to the early conceptual work, except I was operating more physically and more visibly. As this idea developed, I moved into works like *Diamond Cutter's Wedding* where coal was put in slings pulled back like slingshots, aimed at sieves, screens and particle bins. Every one of those elements had a counterpart within the mental construct of art making. The whole idea was to try to hold the idea back, to keep the coal from launching forward, to restrain it from happening. In restraining it, you hallucinated what the result would be. It was a way of saving the idea and hallucinating the structure that could be made by it. Most of this work was based on the suspicion that in making objects, the closer the object comes to completion the further away it gets from the point of origin, the further away it gets from the mind, from its genesis. Objects always appeared cooled down. These works tried to put the heat back in the mechanism, tried to leave tools in the work. If a welding torch was used to construct it, the tendency was to leave it in, to leave remnants of the initiation of the work, the process of its making.

GC Do you feel that the work approaching the beginning of the 80s was an extreme reaction toward the growing interest in painting as manifested in "bad painting" or Neo-expressionism?

DO Work between 1979 and 1983 was so intense that I wasn't distracted by the new painting, the shift in the art world. I wasn't interested in it at the time. I was making large constructions. Here was such a logical and strong core that was so convincingly lined-up with the earlier conceptual work that I felt it to be right. It's interesting to see those moments when the art world shifts to a new alignment in sharp contrast to your own system of beliefs. But I welcomed what appeared to be this perverse move back into painting, because it enriched the profession. If things always move in alignment with your own sensibility, that's too perfect. It's art's characteristic to abandon its practitioners occasionally, to leave them high and dry, to change the definition of what is considered cutting-edge. I think this is all very positive.

GC How do the works of the late 70s connect with the early works in 1967 and 1968?

DO The similarity was in the mindset or the system of ideas. The work in 1979 was based on ten years of conceptualism, but moved to a quasi-architectural mode. This work wasn't as radical as the theoretical work done in 1968. But it was enlarging on an idiom that created new territory. In a work like *Shape Transmission Chamber for the Ultimate Smoke Signal*, I was obsessed with the necessity for sculpture to do something. One problem was how you justify the claim on any object, how can you say the object is yours, how can you say you originated it? It seemed to me that to claim the object you had to draw it through a subterranean body/ mind concourse. This relates to the idea of utter-

Falling Room, *1979*

Exit for the South Bronx, *1979*
Collection of the Museum of Contemporary Art, Los Angeles, California

Detail of Waiting for the Midnight Special (A Thought Collision Factory for Ghost Ships), *1979*

ance, of pulling the utterance out of the body. The other problem was enacting the work, how it engaged the initial idea without losing itself in the material form. The sculpture had to be in the process of becoming. It had to be in an unstable state because as it stabilized it distanced itself too much from the point of initiation. The early structural pieces had elements like conveyor belts, springs, casters, wheels, places where things were pulled up in the air, stretched or hanging. This threw the work into a suspended state of becoming. The machine or factory was a perfect metaphorical construct for structures in a precarious balance between their initiation and their eventual resting place. It made traditional structures that rested on the ground seem relatively inert, untravelled, dormant. I was interested in trying to make sculpture less inert and more in transition.

GC Tell me more about these art-machines. What sort of humanistic content do you see in them? How do they engage the process of art making?

DO I did *Way Station for Launching an Obsolete Power. (A Thought Collision Factory in Pursuit of Journey)* for an exhibition at PS 1. It's a good example of an early machine, which I often talk about as being autobiographical. The piece consisted of a large construction resting on ramps with a conveyor belt going out the window, with templates in the shape of missiles, ready to drop into slits on the top of the roof like toast in a toaster. The templates were tied to cables and the cables were tenuously strung through pulleys, which then seemed to operate on something else. The idea that the work was in transition was extremely important, that the work appeared not finished, but in the process of engagement. Going back to what I said about the utterance, it was as if you couldn't really lay an authoritative claim to anything, you couldn't really originate anything. All you could do was set up a series of potential events, which here involved a series of traps, pulleys, cables, circulating bins, templates and molds. In a way it was a little Duchampian like *The Large Glass*, a group of elements in a mysterious complex. Within it was the mysterious agenda, not clearly defined, but signs of how these things could affect one another. It described facets of the thought process via certain industrial components. In saying those words, "mental process," you can begin to see wheels turning. *Final Stroke. Project for a Glass Factory*, 1980 was made up of numerous elements that had associations to a mental construct. It had doors that would rotate if they were hit, openings, sieves, screens, elevated tracks with materials on sleds that were pulled back and aimed at a central station. It had a crankshaft hovering above that looked like a diagram of a heart attack graph on a medical machine. The sleds were equipped with grinding wheels instead of rubber wheels, implying that they would go down the steel tracks with abrasive motion. Things were always pulled back and harnessed with rubber straps. There were ignition systems with gas-powered devices that introduced temperature, heat into the system. Everything was carefully associated with mental counterparts. These early machine works were always meant to reference the mental complex that was the art idea.

About the same time, I did a piece called *Object with a Memory*, a large construction that looked like a camera, but it was far more complex. It was about

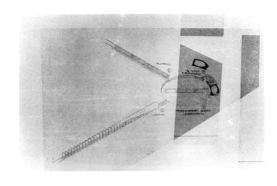

eighteen feet long with hundreds of different elements. I started out with the idea of a recording device which each time it took in an image, it changed its physical form. So if it took a picture of a house its initial shape would extrude and it would develop a peaked roof. If it took a picture of a boat it would include an additional mutation as the house was also wed to the boat. If it snapped a picture of a piece of furniture, that would be compounded as well. So it was a mutation made of numerous inputs, each one affecting the others. Not only did it take in images, it also remembered how they were made, retaining the tools used in making the object. There were legs made from propped up saws, augers and drills, a drum skin that referenced perhaps the retina, lined with hundreds of pencils. This work collected the remnants of both the images it took and the equipment necessary in originating the objects. Fantastic as this machine sounds, I didn't mean for this to be a Goldbergian contraption. The desire was to bring the elements together in a way that would initiate reflection on the mental process.

GC Are there personal elements or meanings embedded in these machines? What about the use of bodily elements?

DO I did parallel *Final Stroke. Project for a Glass Factory* to a relationship, so there may be more to say about that. I was interested in a series of components in a precariously placed complex to describe a fracture in a relationship. I don't know if this was a necessary adornment. *Final Stroke* is about fracture, and it also relates to some of the early Body Art in terms of being about a point of collapse. I wanted to make evident and visible an internal state of chaos, disarray and potential collapse. A lot of this work referenced body systems, aspects of the body. One work used giant bellows to indicate breathing. In front of the bellows were galvanized tunnels which approached crossed tracks, indicating potential collision. This work was similar to the agenda of the early 70s in using the body in a clinical way, very much in service of exploration. The desire to make visible a mental architecture is really related to the impulses of the Body Art agenda in the 70s. It is questionable whether divorce or fracture in relationships add anything to the content of a work like this, but I was trying to shield it from any kind of possible input.
These works existed as extremely visual and complex structures, always driven back to reference an ephemeral thought process or physiological process, especially the throat, the windpipe, breathing, and so on. It was almost as if the self was being laid out on a field of structural elements and put in a transactional episode.

GC These machine works very often seem to imply violence or destruction. What are you trying to convey with this negative energy?

DO These works often were aggressive. That is an aspect that related them to Body Art and even Land Art. I'm not at all interested in sublime, pastoral issues, moving in retreat or in harmony. I prefer to make work that deals with injustice, a troubled area, some negative human condition. I've never been interested in adding to the world of beauty, reinforcing the good, the blessed, the

Drawing for Detail of Waiting for the Midnight Special (A Thought Collision Factory for Ghost Ships), *1979*

Diamond Cutter's Wedding, *1979*
Photo S. Licitra

harmonious. I'm sure this tendency continues in my work today. Often the work has a kind of dark nature that has to be carefully maneuvered so that it doesn't seem unnecessarily verbose and morbid. It's a question of coupling characteristics that are uplifting and optimistic to play on contrast and balance so the works don't fall into the dark abyss.

GC What was the meaning of the fireworks employed in a number of these factory pieces? What did they signify for you?

DO The use of pyrotechnics in the factory complexes around 1981 and 1982 announced the beginning of the end. Making the structures function as armatures, as superstructures for an event, downplayed the credibility of the structures, and directed the attention toward what they could do, their alchemical function. The fireworks in their projecting arcs and lines seemed notational to me, like a language capable of mapping out abstract information. It was as if the launching structures, through the exorcism of the fireworks, were exuding their underlying meaning, what they meant, in this notational, hot language propelling into the sky. I was also interested in the transactional quality of rockets. Unlike pencils, they can collide with other rockets and change their direction, so they are a dynamic drawing force. I knew that this was putting me in a singular domain. The work was so different from the painting that was going on. For a short while I felt like a mad scientist who had become so immersed in his work that he didn't know a major war was going on in the country. Again, I felt seduced by the discovery of an extremely incredible link to past sculpture, yet totally incongruent with what was happening around me in terms of the art world.

GC Talk a little about your friendship with Vito Acconci. Did you share the same thoughts or philosophical approach to art?

DO I met Vito around 1969 and developed a friendship with him. I have had a great respect for his work from that point on. He was moving away from poetry into performance, so I was really very close to him during this early period. His work has remained extraordinarily important. I think he's one of the few artists who continues to be restless and continues to push from year to year, never seeming to relax into any particular mode. We share the view of art continuing to move along, never getting too comfortable or being afraid to take risks. We have similar qualities of spirit in common.

GC Did you collaborate with Acconci on some of the machine works?

DO I did a show at the ICA in Philadelphia with Vito Acconci and Alice Aycock that explored these various machine contraptions, a work called *Occasion for Expansion*, in some ways the most ambitious machine work. It started in a sort of Duchampian way, with couples lying horizontally on hammocks, breathing a mysterious love-gas, after which they would begin to make love and begin to push hammocks up and down, thereby activating a giant bellows. The bellows had pipes and hoses attached to it that would inflate a city made of tires with

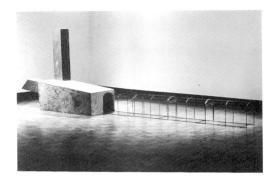

Shape Trasmission Chamber for the Ultimate Smoke Signal, *1979*

Way Station for Launching an Obsolete Power (A Thought Collision Factory in Pursuit of Journey), *1979*

Final Stroke. Project for a Glass Factory, *1980*
Photo Ben Blackwell, San Francisco
San Francisco Museum of Modern Art, San Francisco, California, Gift of Warner Communications Inc.

Object with a Memory, *1983*
Photo Serra Di Felice Gallery, New York
Munson-Williams Proctor Institute, Museum of Art, Utica, New York

giant pipes that protruded from the center hole. It looked like giant bagpipes. Hundreds of small tubes went from one to the another, indicating a procedural inflation, a building of this inflated, dream city. The final element was a giant airship that was poised on a labyrinthian steel armature, which held a giant basket. The airship was presumably an offshoot of this inflated city. The subtitle of this work is *A Combat of Structural Projections*. The tubes and pipes brought energy into the airship, which in real terms was being inflated by a stream of hot air from an enormous butane gas jet. So it was a giant hot air balloon, but it was in the shape of an atomic mushroom cloud. Hovering above the bagpipes were brass cymbals that were tied to pulleys, capable of hovering above and coming down, thereby stopping the airflow, potentially causing the city to collapse. These cymbals were controlled by the airship, so this hallucinated transactional structure was operating in a cybernetic exchange of cerebral combat where the inflation created by the couples making love was capable of being stifled, smothered, and thereby collapsing the city and endangering the airship. This piece represented the beginning of the end, losing consciousness of the implications of what I was doing, of engaging materials and combustible elements and making something that grew beyond the size of the gallery, that had transactional interdependent elements that function or dysfunction in chaotic exchange.

GC Of what importance are drawings to you? How do you see them, as ways of throwing out ideas, or technical material for building works? Are they non-physical forms, immaterial or dematerialized sculpture?

DO Not to downplay the drawings, but they operate in a secondary position to my work. Drawings are only primary documents, remnants of an early idea force, the first lines indicating the materialization of an image. So a drawing can be primary, but my primary drawings have always been cryptic and illegible. They were the kind of drawings I did in a bar on a napkin and lost the next day. Most of my drawings are done after the idea has cooled down somewhat. These don't represent the initial stage, as the idea is already crystal clear. Often they are done after the work is built. Some drawings are a prelude to the work, so they have immediacy about them. The architectural drawings used to build a work are cold. The primary or immediate drawing I've mentioned is similar to projective verse, where the utterance is drawn from a deep region and brought out in its first emission. You can't approach with intention, you can't want it to happen. When I engage drawing nowadays it's a bit uncomfortable — it's not what I do. It's something that's used to communicate easily within the art system, that's manageable. Clearly in a way my heart isn't in it enough to make it a primary function.

Newton Discovering Gravity, *Artpark, New York, 1984*

Occasion for Expansion. A Combat of Structural Projections, *1981*
Photo Wayne Cozzolino, Philadelphia, Pennsylvania

GC At the end of the 80s a number of works deal with change and transformation in everyday objects. What interested you about dissecting and reassembling these objects, creating divergent territories?

DO In 1988 I was drawn to the fact that an object like a baseball bat could be cut in half on the long axis and swung into an arc, where the space between the two halves could be filled with static, which I silkscreened onto fiberglass. It's as if the bat solidified the way it went. This tendency to elongate and solidify the passage of things is true of *Wake Collision*, which is a boat that splits in two. The halves move in opposite directions, the space in between is filled in, creating another boat. So this boat is capturing its journey of separation. Not only it is solidifying its separation, it's colliding with what appears to be another boat, but it's not a boat it's the mid-section; the journey of the boat propped up on top of the structure. I was trying to make visible the passages of objects and also create an incident within a journey.

GC What about objects based on fundamental errors or mistakes? What interests you in these false events, documented in such works as *Black Pool* or *Windmill*?

DO Black Pool is in the exhibition in Venice. It is simply a constructed pool table with a hypothetical game in which a hit ball missed the hole, so you could call that a mistake. This mistake was expanded not only across the surface of the table, but three-dimensionally using steel rods. This mistake created an armature, a construct. Not only did this mistake occur on top of the table, it created the architecture and design of the table itself, which looks like some kind of molecular structure. The legs are giant bowling balls set in another atomic structure, all based on a mistake. A recent work *Windmill* uses a reference that's quite different, that is the idea of stuttering. The words "stitch, ditch, bitch, dyke" are mounted on the wall. The beginning these words elongated, as though they're stuttered. A windmill made out of a kitsch fabric found in Holland spins in front of the words and blurs them. I was very interested in the physiological problem of stuttering, because on one hand I saw it as a way of creating a new word. Some dysfunction, some lack of mechanical function made these words hard to say. This interested me a lot. I began to think of what happens in stuttering and applied it to objects, making a stuttered object, an object that was hard to make happen.

GC What is the role of dark emotions like fear and danger in your recent works? How does it function in a work like *Murder in Hawaiian Shirts*, 1989?

DO I've mentioned before that I am not driven to make a work about the sublime or the beautiful. There are many reasons for this. An artist's life can be extremely contemplative, introspective. This condition seems to create a secret alliance that makes dark content more accessible, more intriguing. I would be suspicious talking to a happy artist. I'm not sure I'd be terribly interested in what they had to say. Depression is something that seems to figure often in art making, although I don't know that good art is made during anything like clinical depression. It's almost a shamanistic immersion into self-darkness which gives me something usable, something I can reference. There are many writers, poets and artists who would claim these episodes have given them perspective, insight and strength. It doesn't mean you're focusing on society's dark side. I really don't harbor a constant view of the world as one of an irreparable vortex of oblivion.

Murder in Hawaiian Shirts, 1989, is really a work about photography. It consists of two giant torsos clothed in extremely loud, bright shirts with images of animals, fish, sharks, sailboats and the like that have been silkscreened onto the fabric. They're about four or five feet high. The silkscreen images have been coupled with the actual images, so a shark would be photographed and silkscreened, and the actual shark would be positioned on the shirt. The two shirts face one another, and on the floor between the Hawaiian shirts, the three dimensional sharks actually attack one another. It's about taking the artifice out of photography and upending it to a dimension that becomes more believable, more concrete.

GC How has your sensibility developed over time? Do you see more or less direct connections between your early conceptual work and the recent sculpture?

DO I was talking to students from France the other day and I launched into a tirade, trying to make a big impression on them that conceptual art was really very, very old. I dwelled on the fact that the conceptual movement that seems to be so ubiquitous now, so influential, comes from thirty years ago. However, I'm not aware of the degree of conceptual orientation in this new work. I have travelled these orbits so often that it's very hard to trace. Making work that spontaneously self-destructs and burns its bridges makes it hard to claim firm historical lineage from those early days. I'm not aware of doing something that purposely wants to confront the mechanisms that were part of the work from 1968. At the same time in 1968 I would not have made *Pear Eating Pumpkin*. The work has travelled quite a distance to get where it is now. The way the recent works are materializing can change, and I'm hoping for change. Change can't be forced. I learned that years ago. You can't force yourself to see through a wall, you can't force yourself successfully to make the work better. It's a simple desire, but difficult to achieve. Making the work better means making the work better all around. The things that feed the momentum leading to a new opening can only be laid out on the table the way they come. The orders come in at their own pace, as with an unprofessional waiter.

GC Your work rarely makes reference to art history, yet *Revolving Kissing Racks*, 1990, very blatantly engages Duchamp. What is your relationship to earlier art historical movements? How do these ideas influence you?

DO *Revolving Kissing Racks* involved two giant Duchampian bottle racks with what looks like Man Ray-like lips, very large plastic lips which hang from the rack hooks. They revolve, coming into very close contact with one another, almost brushing one lip against the other as they revolve. It is unusual for me to be so quotational, referring to Duchamp and Man Ray. This is not something that I do easily, and I only do it rarely. I don't get much energy from hooking into other art so blatantly. I harbor this fantasy and I know it is a fantasy, that art is materialized by a combination of strong subterranean urges and a mysterious field of seduction that connects with primal forces, creating the urge to concertize and communicate. This is all a hysterical fantasy, but at the same time it is so ingrained in me that when I try to apply an idea from outside this circuit, it doesn't work. Using art to service something else doesn't work. To use it to instigate some art historical reference doesn't seem to push the art far enough. A work like *Revolving Kissing Racks* really operates with simple, universal relationships. Sure, it uses a Duchampian bottle rack, sure, the lips might refer to another artist, but basically the impulse came from the fact that the lips on the lower part of the rack come very close together. The lips on top are far apart. It's the feeling of this condition that interests me most.

GC What about the Surrealistic element? Is it a way of peering into the unknown?

DO Some of the recent work has been read as having Surrealistic overtones. I'm sure there is something to that idea in some cases. But Surrealism never really interested me because the ideas behind it, like automatic writing, dreams, etc. aren't really from the world that I know. I was born in 1938, and grew up during Abstract Expressionism and there was a different kind of tension because of that. Surrealism was something that really didn't cross my path. I can see how you'd read some of the pieces that do have exaggerated mutational elements as relating to Surrealism, but I can assure you that it does not come from a conscious alignment with the art historical movement.

GC But what about Pop imagery — several of the works of the 90s seem to refer to a certain Pop attitude, an almost Disney narrative iconography. How do you relate this work to the Pop movement?

DO It's true that certain people have mentioned this Pop attitude in some of the work. I can't explain it really. There seems to be certain content that can be addressed relatively straightforwardly and there's some content that doesn't seem to work that way. In other words, if you use the obvious materials and simply go directly toward that idea, it turns out to be too heavy, its balance is off, it's overkill. Subliminally or intuitively, a lot of the work I make seems to ask for an altered state requiring that certain things be done to the object — occasionally it is increased in size, inflated in some way or another, overstated in caricature, which can come across as a certain Pop sensibility. There are different approaches to sculpture. For instance, there's art that uses raw, natural materials, and tries to make the idea function with a sense of integrity about the material. There's another art that is much more extreme than mine, that does purposely delve into this overblown reference to commercialism, reference to cartoon characters, things of this sort which would be impossible for me. I operate somewhere between these two states. Most of the materials I use are natural, a tendency that comes from Land Art, from Body Art. If I use a brick, it's a real brick. But occasionally something happens and I feel the need to make a very large bone out of plaster or a very large pumpkin with eyes and a nose and a mouth. You just work with materials a certain way, and the rest is given over to constant scanning and reassessment with a view to new applications.

GC How do you see the relationship between your work and some of the other artists in the 80s and 90s working with assemblage, like Stockholder and Rhoades? Do you see a difference in attitude between the generations? Is there a common process of deconstruction?

DO I think both Stockholder and Rhoades are doing very good work. I appreciate the hands-on element in their work. It has strong roots in early installation but it's a spin on the subject. It's a good example of a valid extension of that work. There were certainly precedents by Morris and others of installations that changed daily, where the material was distributed, that lead to what Stockholder is doing now. But she is getting results in the way she applies formalist painting and the more handicraft elements of art making to create a quasi-satirical formalist installation. It resonates. Likewise, Rhoades' work is an extension of the idea of leaving tools in the work, remnants of the process, but he gives it a large and frenzied treatment. Concentrating on the fragments, there's no beginning or end to it. This is a very valid assault against the discrete object. The word "deconstruction" wasn't being used in 1968. When we got into that area, we'd say something about Structuralism or semiotics as a method of interrogating language and meaning. We didn't know about people like Derrida and Baudrillard at that point. But there was a great intuitive feeling about the notion of deconstruction in the mid-70s — using clinical interrogation of art to magnify the self, to expose the self. This was very much a form of deconstruction. It unfolded in the 80s and became ubiquitous. Suddenly it seemed one could claim that everybody was operating in a deconstructivist mode. People like Sherrie Levine and Louise Lawler certainly launched a deconstruction of early conceptual art. This whole second generation group found great problems with the way the early conceptual art was being presented. The claims that it made for credibility and legitimacy in terms of documentation troubled them. Of course this position took the burn out of conceptual art, took the fire out of it, gave it over to easy transmission, more successful transmission. It would have been improbable that early conceptual art could have had its eyes on the ground ahead and also the cold, analytical temperament of these later artists.

GC Are we going through a catastrophic process now of decomposition, of dissipation, where the differences between the live body and the artificial body are evaporating?

DO If there was ever a time in history for this to happen, I would say it could happen now. We are bombarded with the visual replication of the human body, with this focus on fashion and on adornment and various treatments for the body, having your nails cleaned. All this makes the body a kind of mannequin, walking around waiting for these things to be done to it. This is a perfect time for this kind of deconstruction to occur. Certainly there's a case for the idea of the cyborg. Individuals are becoming progressively more superficial, their obedience is being more easily manipulated. There's not much difference anymore between the real and the artificial. The late 50s when all the coffee shops in San Francisco were filled with people discussing what they misunderstood about Existentialism, seems light years away now. Then people lived in a kind of naiveté, with little interest in adornment, in taking care of oneself. These things were not important. As they have become more and more important, this sense of artificiality has increased. As the body concentrates more on itself, it becomes more like what it idealizes, which now is usually some kind of mannequin.

GC Sometimes you turn that mode on its head, however, as in *Two Objects*, 1989, where inanimate objects seem to desire the life of a human relationship.

DO *Two Objects* is a piece that consists of two chairs that are moving back and forth into one another, copulating. The fantasy is that the stationary, covered chair is being invaded by a chair of a different style, like it's a different species. The orgasmic exchange between them implies that something may be produced by this. It's about genetic invasion.

GC Your work seems to resist the coolness of the cyborg, however. There is a fever in its creation, even a demonic or trance possession that seems to take over, which shows the nakedness of your reality. How do you understand the visionary capacity of making the work?

DO The other day I gave a lecture and I caught myself saying that the best state of mind for making art is like a dimly lit room. It's where you can't see everything in harsh reality, things are vague. I like to enter into a work with a shadow cast across my mind, because if there are bright lights in every nook and cranny, you can become immobile. It can seem that every move you make has already been done. You can find billions of reasons not to do it, there seems to be a high probability of failure. You box yourself in. The answer is not to turn all the lights out, hoping that by not seeing anything you can make anything credible either. In the partially darkened space I prefer to develop a visual hum, a murmur that reduces and absorbs the surrounding field of intrusion. It creates a chamber of concentration within which you can work.

GC Your work often uses soft materials like latex or rubber, tissue or fabric — is this another dialectical condition, where you are always dealing with opposites?

DO I'm sure there is a dialectical superstructure. I've often been criticized as a sculptor for making works out of impermanent materials, materials related more to theater. But frankly I'm much more comfortable when I'm surrounded by assistants who have had experience working for theater because they are capable of instigating something in front of you very quickly. They have a fluid, transactional way of making something happen almost immediately with materials that seem quite suitable to that process, which almost never means steel or cast bronze. Coming from conceptual art, an art that was dematerialized, I am sometimes hesitant to put the things in heavy gauge. Even the factory pieces that were made out of steel were skeletal, they had a lot of mesh and perforated steel, they wanted to be kind of transparent. I know this is part of the sensibility of making the work atmospheric, capturing the idea where it came from, this geyser of steam protruding from your brain. I often use fabric and lightweight or transparent materials as a result. Relatively few works operate in anything close to a monolithic form.

Image Dissonance - Coffee Cup, which will be shown in Venice in an altered form, belongs to this family of works that have a difficult time existing in solid form. It's an image blowing apart in a kind of molecular storm. The elements are zipping across the floor, held by steel rods - these "bounces" are the object as it disintegrates into its component molecules. I appreciate instability, the mutability of things that are capable of this transconfiguration. This relates to so many tributaries in my earlier work, this feeling of the improbability of pinning something down. This probably relates to my general psychopathic career orientation, where I don't have the faith to create a signature style. I'm hesitant to believe any work is radiant enough or able to cast a large enough net that would entrance me enough to make myself its disciple for the rest of my life, perpetuating it.

GC Randomness plays a role in works like *Figure Skating*, 1990. It seems to be going out of control visually, a vortex of activity which enacts a loss of control. How did this work come about?

DO In *Figure Skating* there is a hypnotic condition physically as you're swirling around the ice going in circles. For a year leading into the piece, I was somewhat obsessed with the figure of 8,000,000. Every time I sat down or had a piece of paper in my hand, I would scribble out 8 million, 8 and six zeros over and over again. I envisioned these zeros as being out of control. There is a sort of uncontrolled, unstoppable motion that finally describes an event. I think subliminally if it references anything in the real world, it's probably the Holocaust.

GC In what ways do you think you might incorporate your work, which already has such an architectural basis, into someone else's architecture? Are you interested in collaborating with sculpturally oriented architects like Frank Gehry?

DO I still don't know to what extent the public art idea will take hold in my work. The last time I thought about this issue was thirty years ago, doing art in the landscape. At that time, architecture was not as radiant as it is now. Thirty years ago, architects were really the enemy. Today there are architects like Frank Gehry who have strong ties to sculpture and probably conceptual and minimal ideas as well. I'm not sure how I will find a rapport with this new architecture. Even though I am showing about thirty models of outdoor pieces in Venice. I haven't yet developed the intense, heart-felt urgency for work to cling, hang, invade, marry with somebody else's architectural master plan. Coming from Land Art, which is a subversive orientation, the tendency is not to join in harmony with an architectural master plan as much as to disrupt it. I don't know if I'm going to be able to successfully eliminate or adapt those impulses. They've been with me for so many years.

GC Since 1995 your interest has turned toward creating more sculptural architectural works for public space. What are your feelings on public art in general, and how do you see your work fitting into these public spaces?

DO For years I was disinterested in so-called public art. I felt that my most successful period in that context was Land Art. Things were economically feasible, you only did what you could afford, what you could arrange. There was a certain primitive feature to that, and my experience in engaging formal commissions that had to be arbitrated and mediated through numerous people, resulted in works that were mostly unsuccessful. For years I felt that work requiring a collaboration with any kind of community board, any kind of art council, like the Public Art Fund, was going to ensure a weak work. Issues come and go, and there was a conscious decision on my part to try again. What's behind this is something more important. As we're moving into the year 2000, there is more potential than ever for transacting a work in public space. This may be a domain that looks good simply because everything else looks so bad. Public art has certainly been a receptacle for some of the worst sculpture ever made, but somehow it seems to have an opening that doesn't exist within the clutches of the art world circuit of museums and galleries.

Works

Second Generation Image. Iron/Boat, 1988

Second Generation Appliance Spirit #3, 1988

p. 60-61
Second Generation Image (Zebra), 1988   *Burnt Rainbow, 1988*

Dead Beats, 1988   *Virus, 1988*   p. 64-65
Image Dissonance. Coffee Cup, 1988

Thought Bones from Between the Fingers of
Fear, 1988

Above the Wall of Electrocution, 1989

Bad Cells are Comin', 1989

Badly Tuned Cow, 1989

Spirit Notes, 1989   Two Objects, 1989   **73**

Functioning Faces, 1990

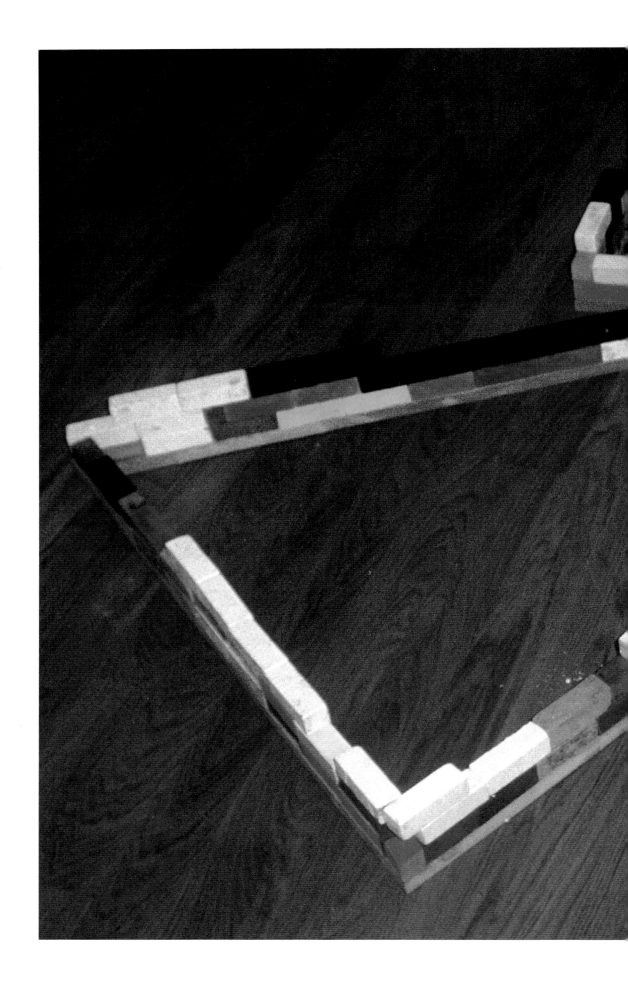

Woman with Halo, 1989

Cross Town Tremors, 1989

Black Pool, 1990

Digestion, 1989

p. 82-83
*Buttermilk Run (ceiling) Digestion. Gypsum
Gypsies (floor)*, 1989

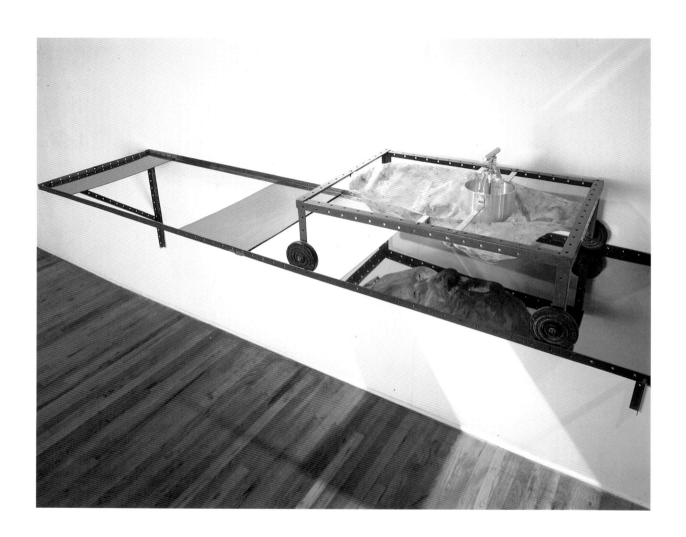

Hot Vomit Machine, 1989   *Slow Clap for Satie*, 1989

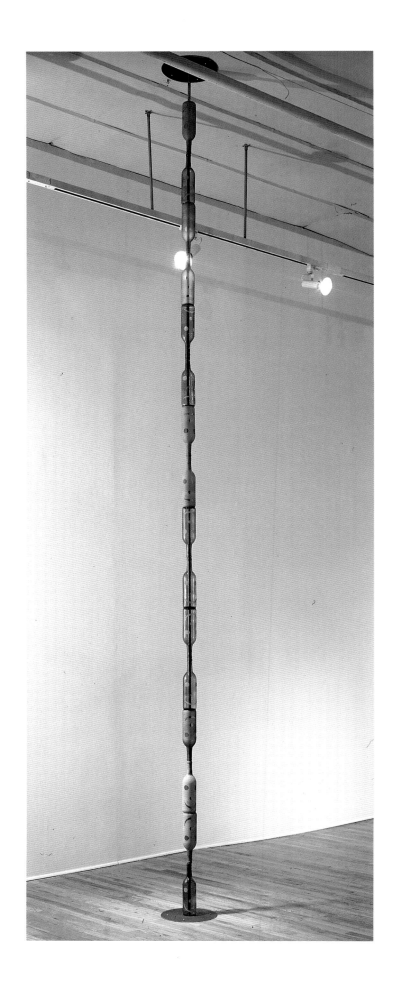

Summit to Sadness, 1989

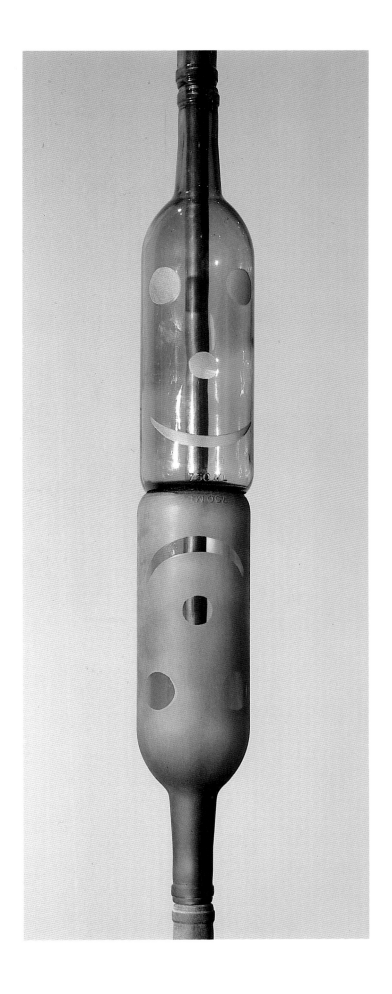

Cutting Tool (From the Power Tool Series),
1989

*Four Spinning Dancers (From the Power
Tool Series),* 1989

Shakers with Shakes, 1989

Five Spinning Dancers (From the Power Tool Series), 1989

Disco Mattress (From the Power Tool Series), 1989

p. 96-97
Aw-ful Waffle, 1991

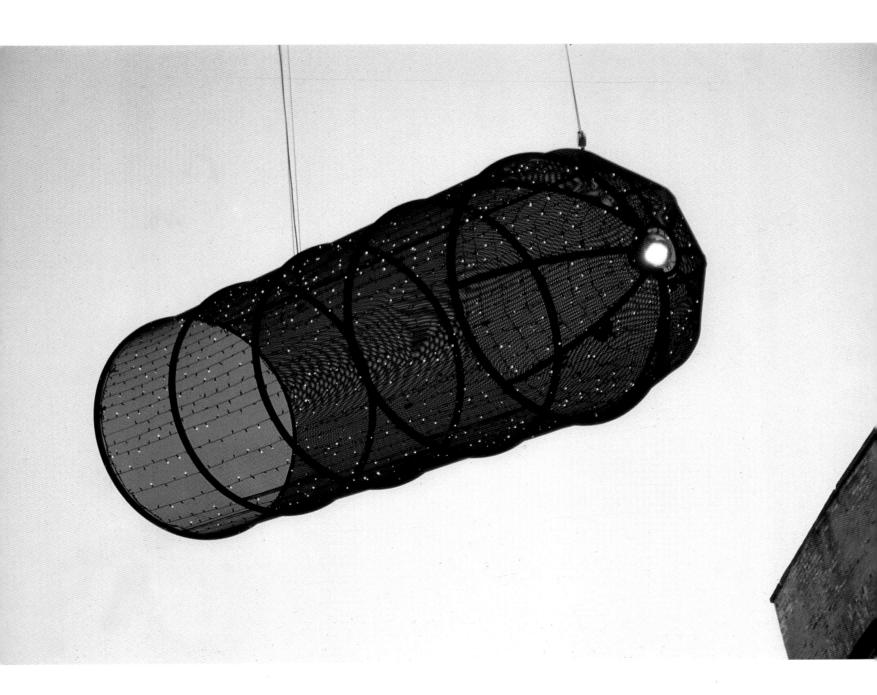

*Between Drinks (floor) Double Headed
Woman with Floating Hearts (wall), 1991*

*Double Headed Woman with Floating
Hearts, 1991*

Vibrating Figures (From the Power Tool Series), 1990

Slave Cactus, 1991   *Figure Skating, 1990*   p. 110-111
                                                                                      Installation, 1990

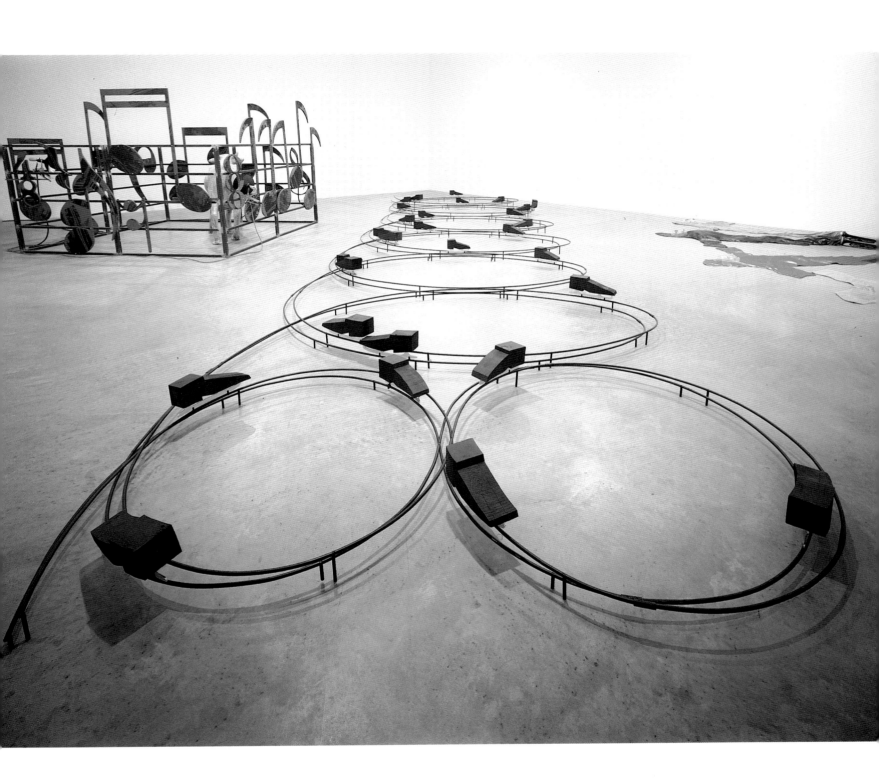

Toe to Heel. Woman Trapped in a Man's Body, 1990

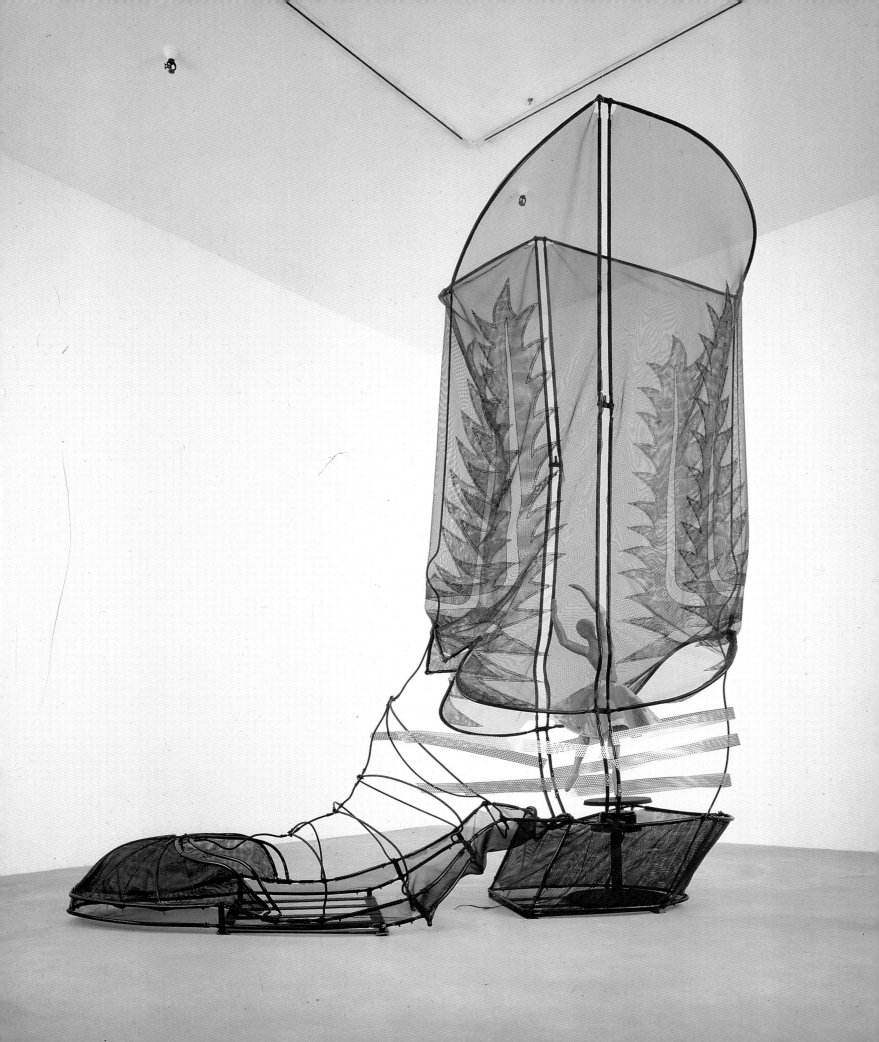

Untitled Wall Piece, 1990   *Combined Expressions, 1991*

Kissing Racks, 1990

p. 120-121
Black, 1991

Upper Cut, 1992

Black Dog in Cage, 1992

p. 128-129
Digestion. Gypsum Gypsies, 1989

Long Distance Anger, 1992   *Tempest in a Teacup, 1992*   p. 132-133
Installation, 1992

Wal-nuts, 1992

p. 136-137
Lungs with Brushes Heart with Paper Liver
with Pencils, 1992

Think Tanks, 1993

Heavy Dog Kiss, 1993

p. 142-143
Galloping through the Wheat, 1993

Sweet Wars, 1993

p. 146-147

Gathering, 1993

Divorce, 1993

Starmen, 1993

Kick, 1993

p. 150-151
Bed Piece, 1993

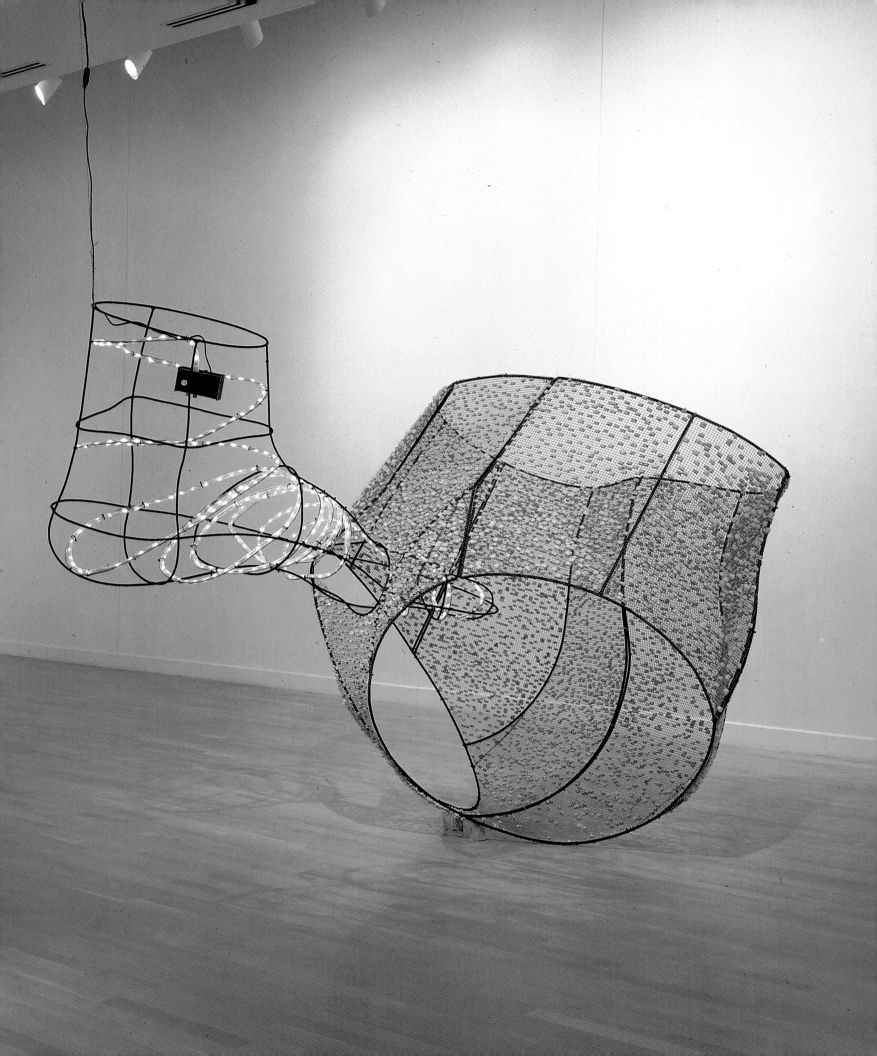

Beasts from Canal Street, 1993

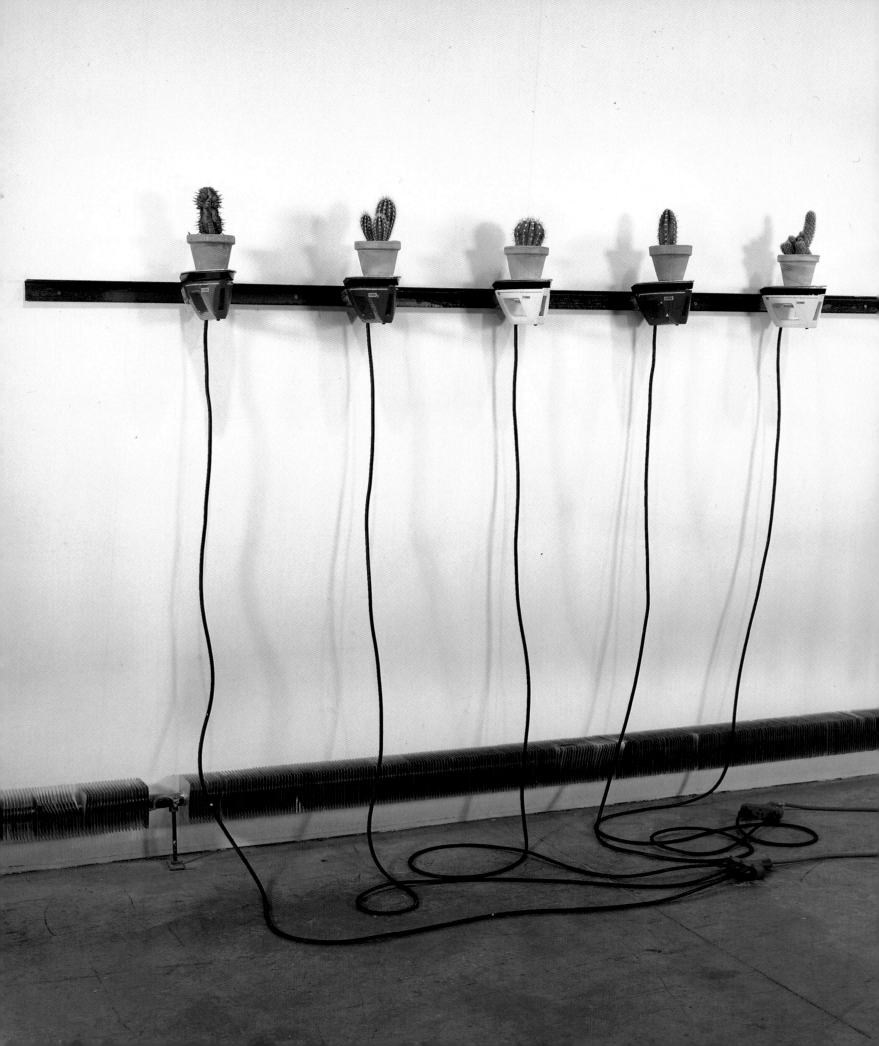

Iron/Cactus, 1994   *Clothed Organ,* 1994

Battered Tears, 1994

Circle Puppets, 1994   *Hot Tattoos*, 1994   p. 160-161
                                                                                  Stutter Pen, 1994

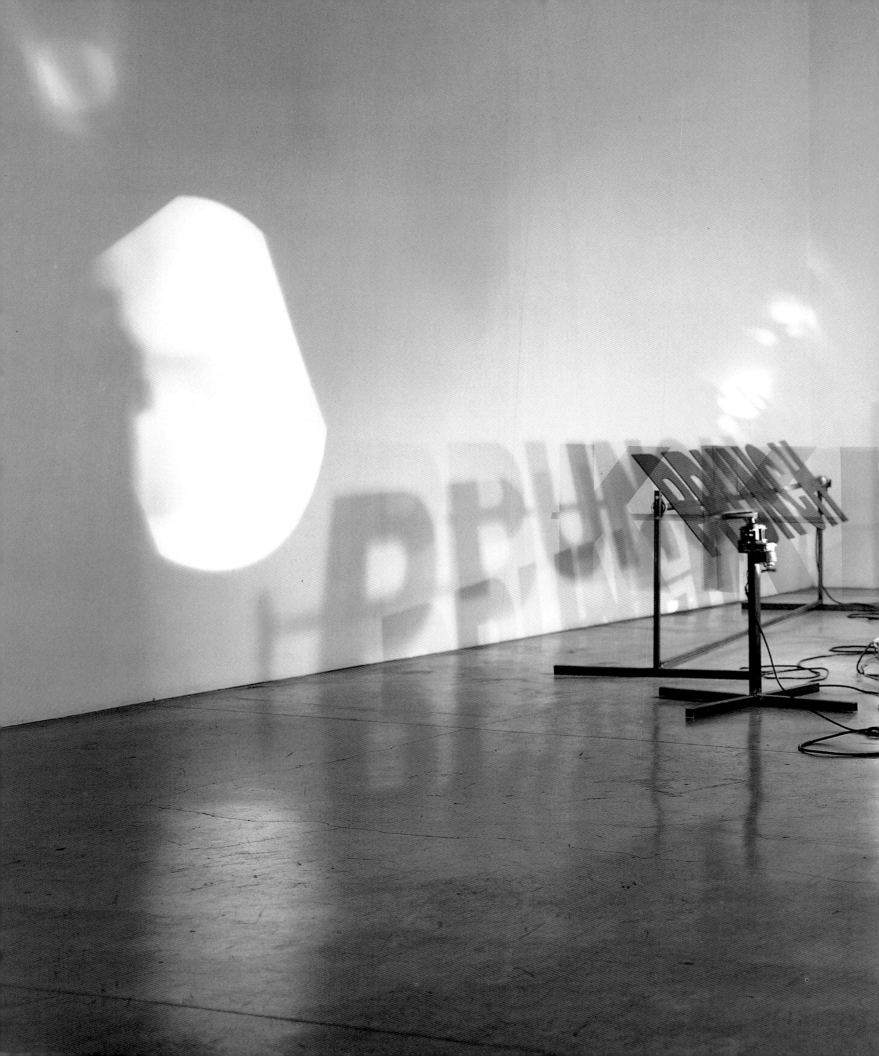

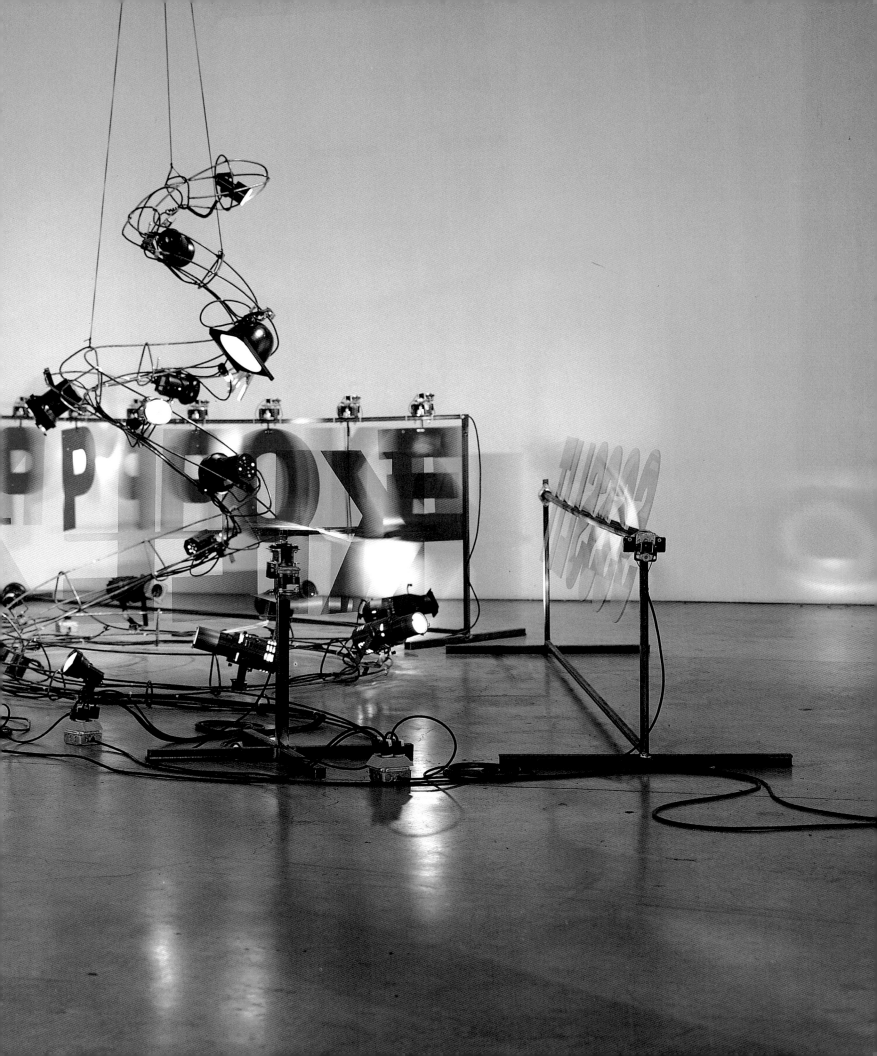

The Last Dance Installation, 1994

The Last Dance, 1994

Spinning Shark, 1994

Untitled, 1993

Finger Churches, 1994

p. 170-171
Blue Tattoo, 1993

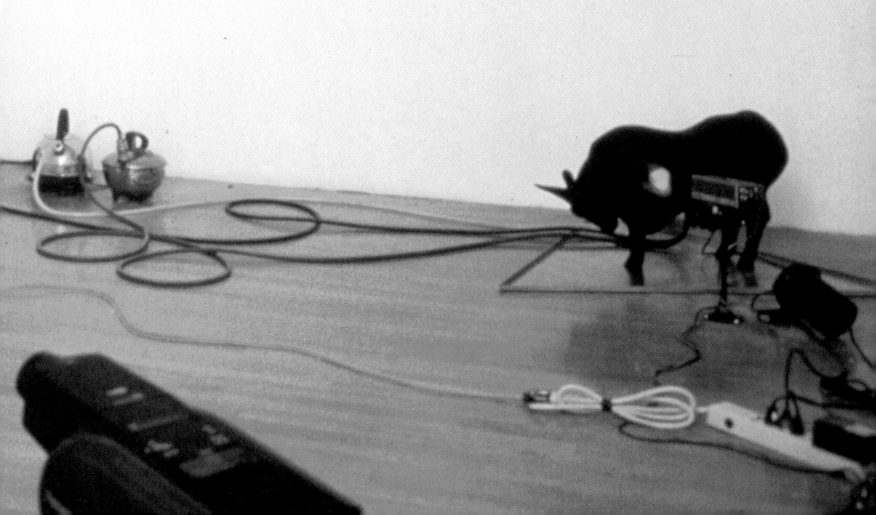

Untitled. Drum Accompaniment, 1993   *Silver Tears,* 1995

Incident at Stutter Pond, 1994

Incident at Stutter Pond, 1994

p. 178-179
Incident at Stutter Pond, 1994

Wolf Trucks: Mobile Land Activators, 1994   *Woman with Cubist Tendencies,* 1993

Love/Hate, 1995

p. 184-185
Windmill, 1995

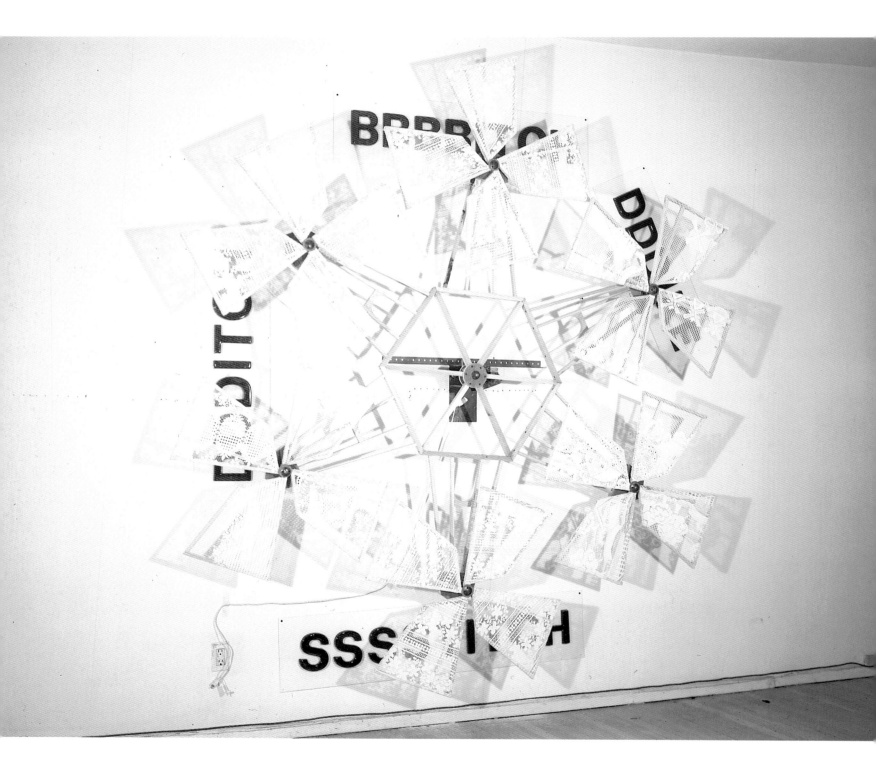

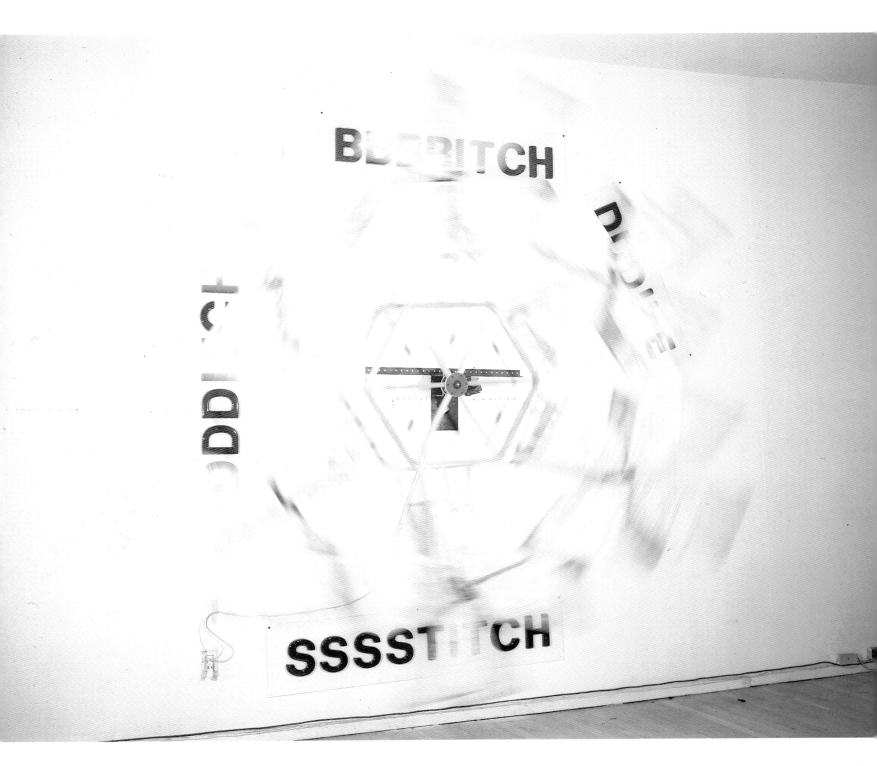

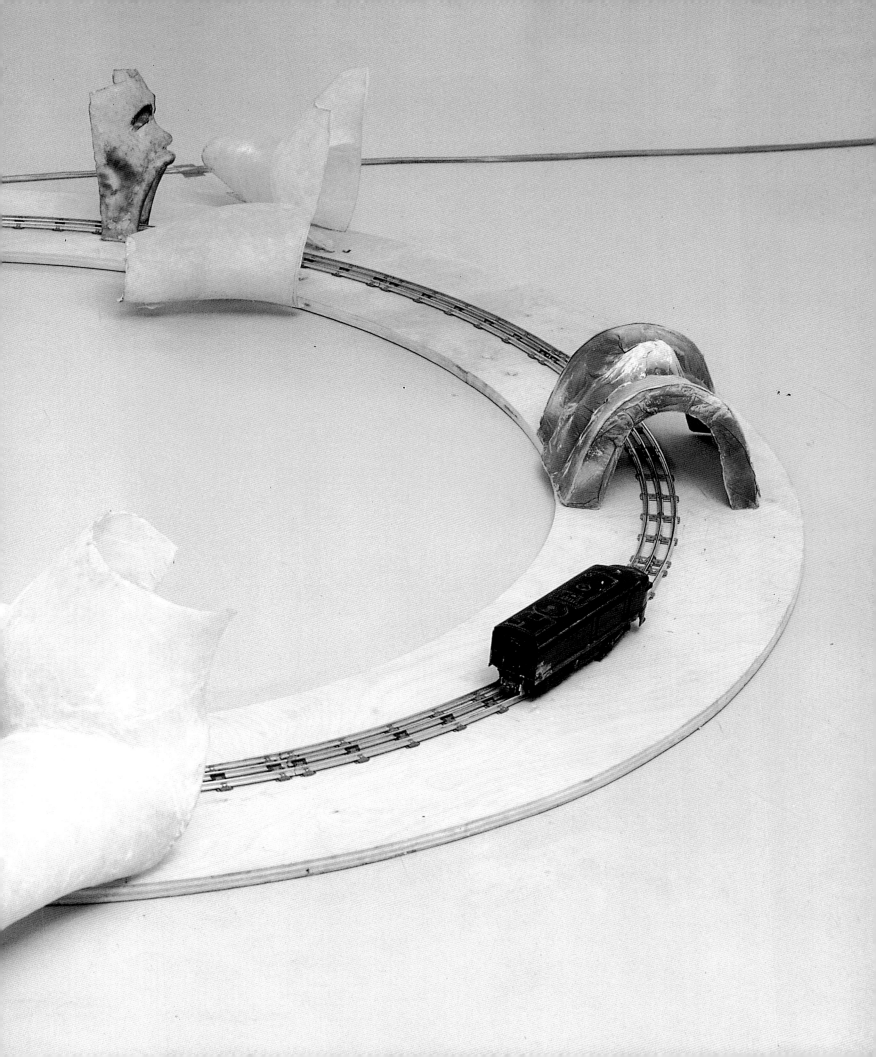

p. 186-187
The Old in and Out, 1995

Earmuffs, 1995

Black Ball, 1995

Chair/Pool, 1996   *Campfire, 1995*   **193**

Color Mix, 1995   *Incubator with Spinning Trees,* 1995

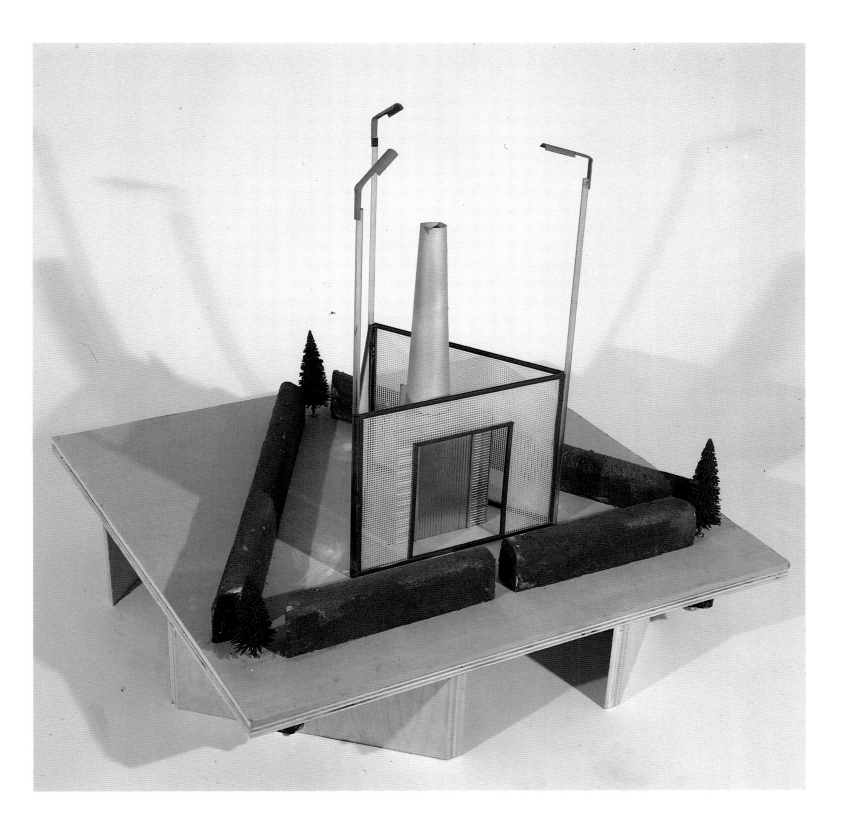

Project for a Lake, 1995

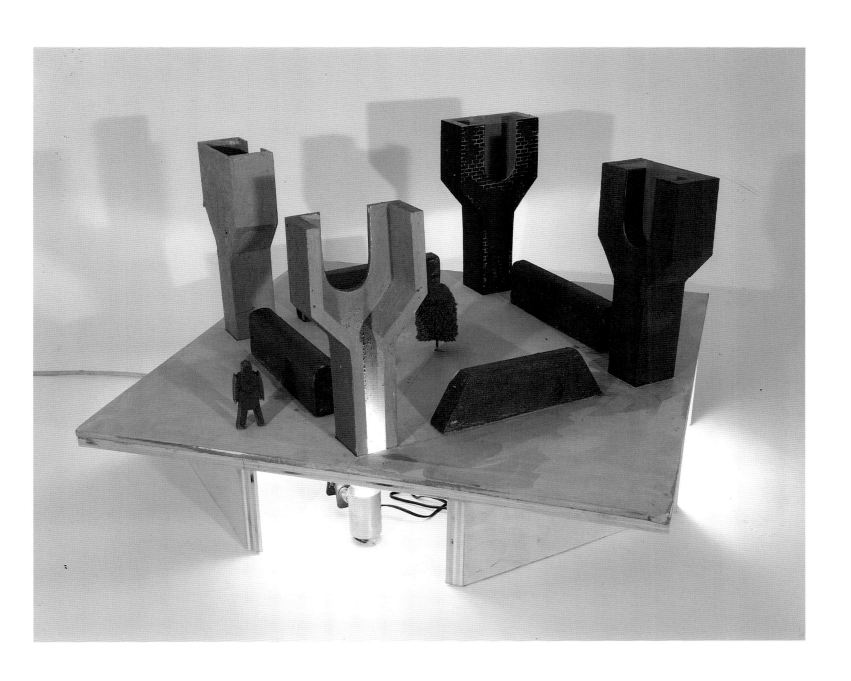

Four Chimneys with Ground Based Sodium Vapor Lights, 1995

Outdoor Proposal with Concrete Curtains,
Angled Bleachers, Hedges with Spinning
Trees, 1995

Vertical Pool, 1995

p. 200-201
Submerged Faces, 1995

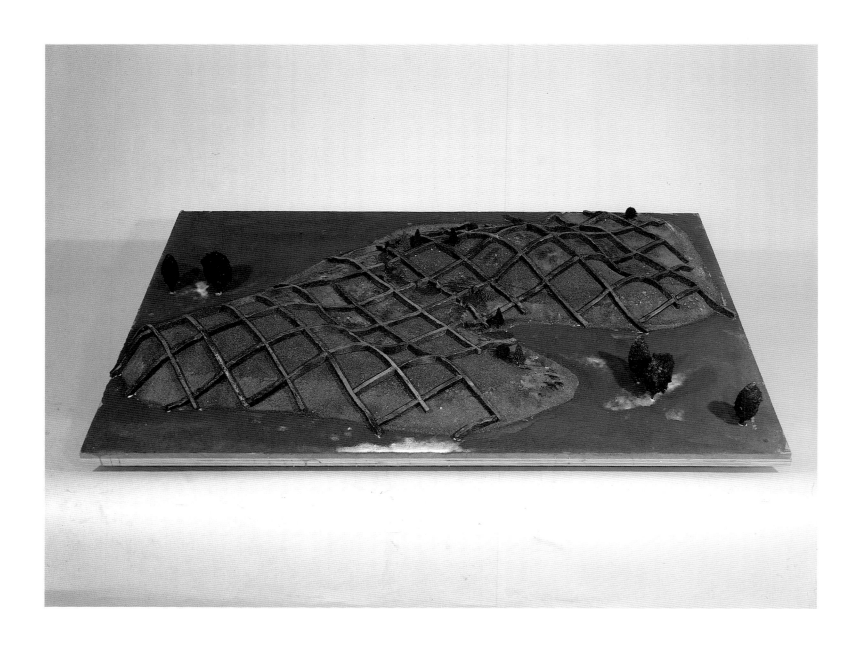

Land Net, 1995

Tulip Run-a Jogging Course, 1995

p. 204-205
Suburban Drift, 1995

203

Rabbit Factory, 1995   *Chair/Pool,* 1995

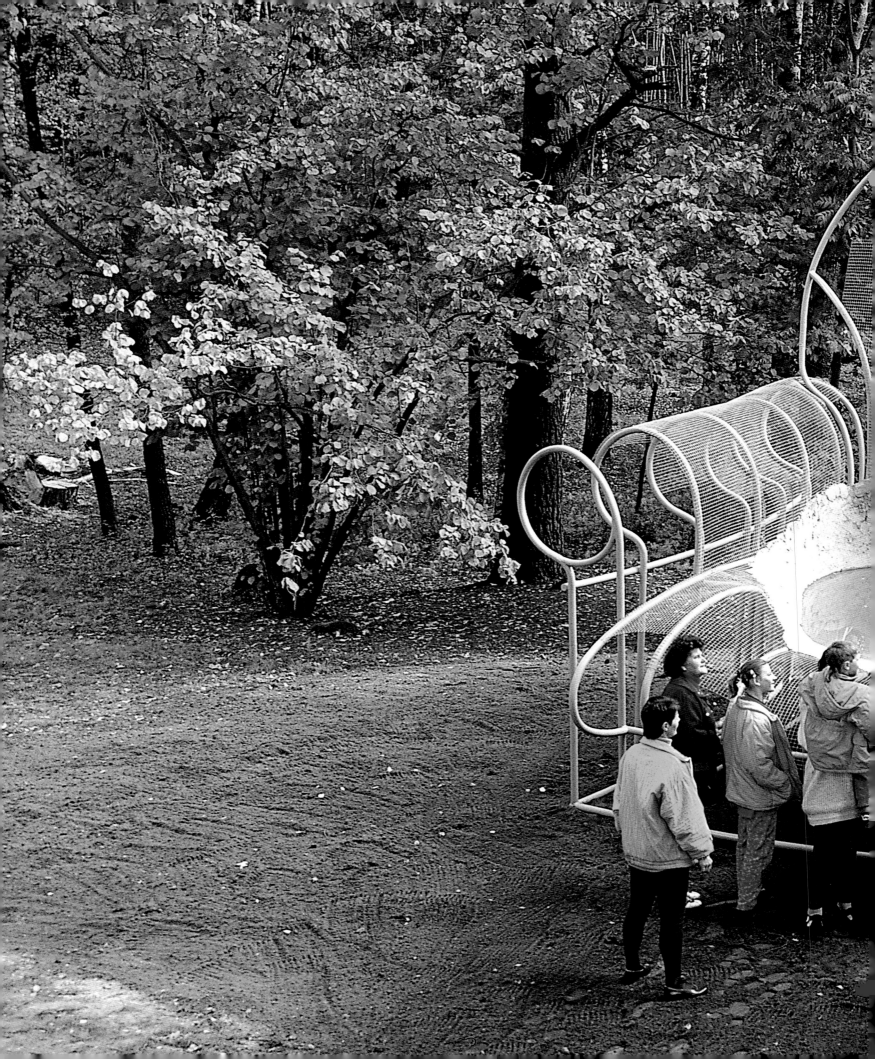

Rabbit Factory, 1995

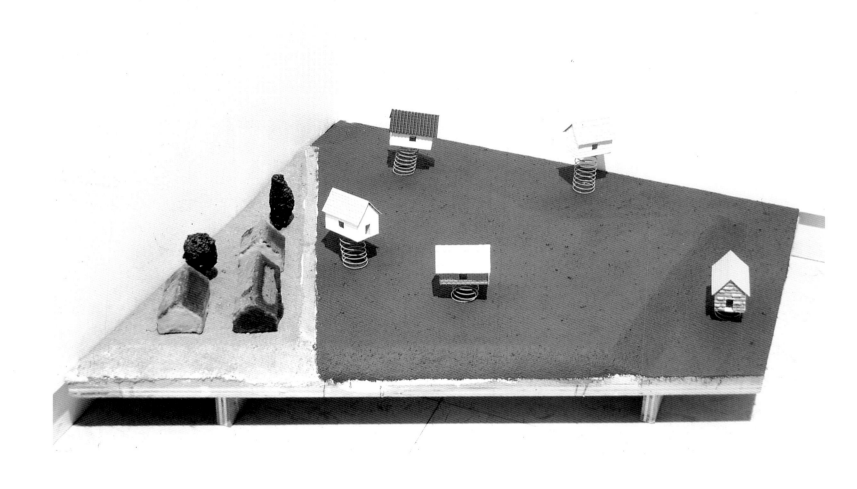

Tornado Houses, 1996

Ski Houses, 1996

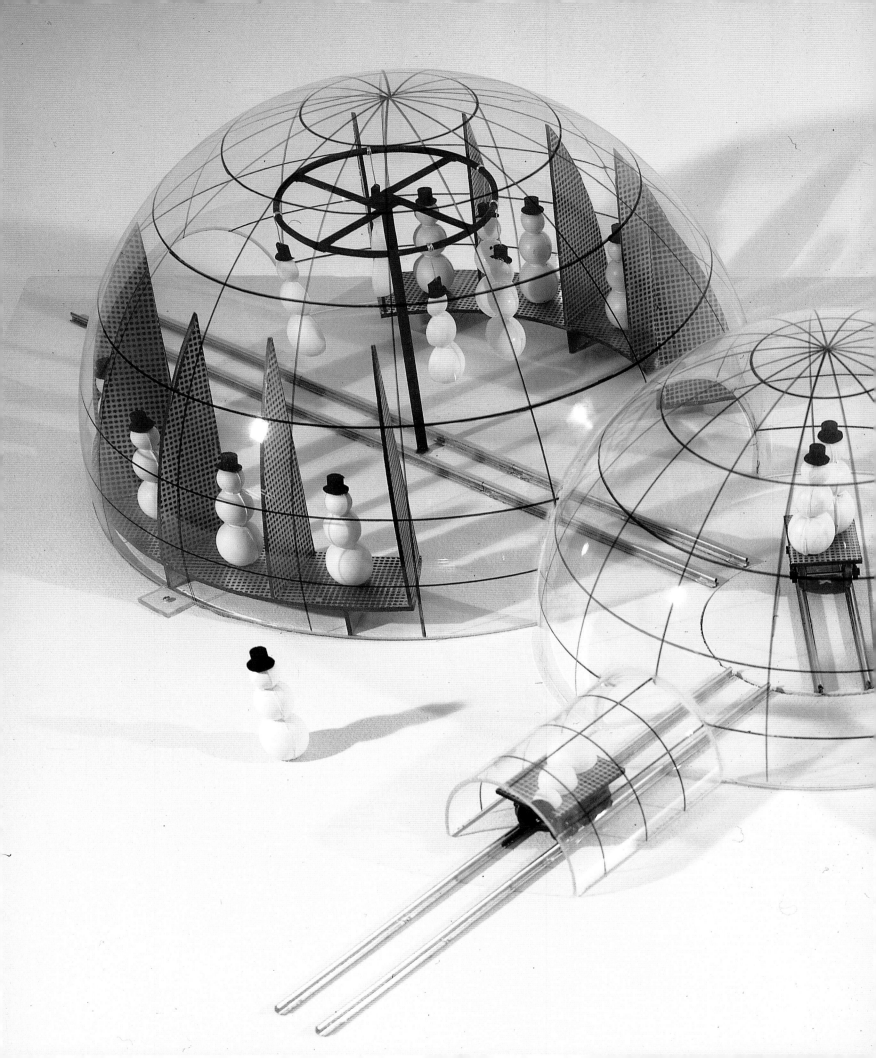

Engagement, 1996

Engagement, 1996

p. 222-223
Four Cornered Murder, 1996

Topiary Piece, 1996

Tar Roses, 1996

Blushing Machine, 1996

Untitled, 1996

p. 232-233
A Ring for Every Finger, 1996

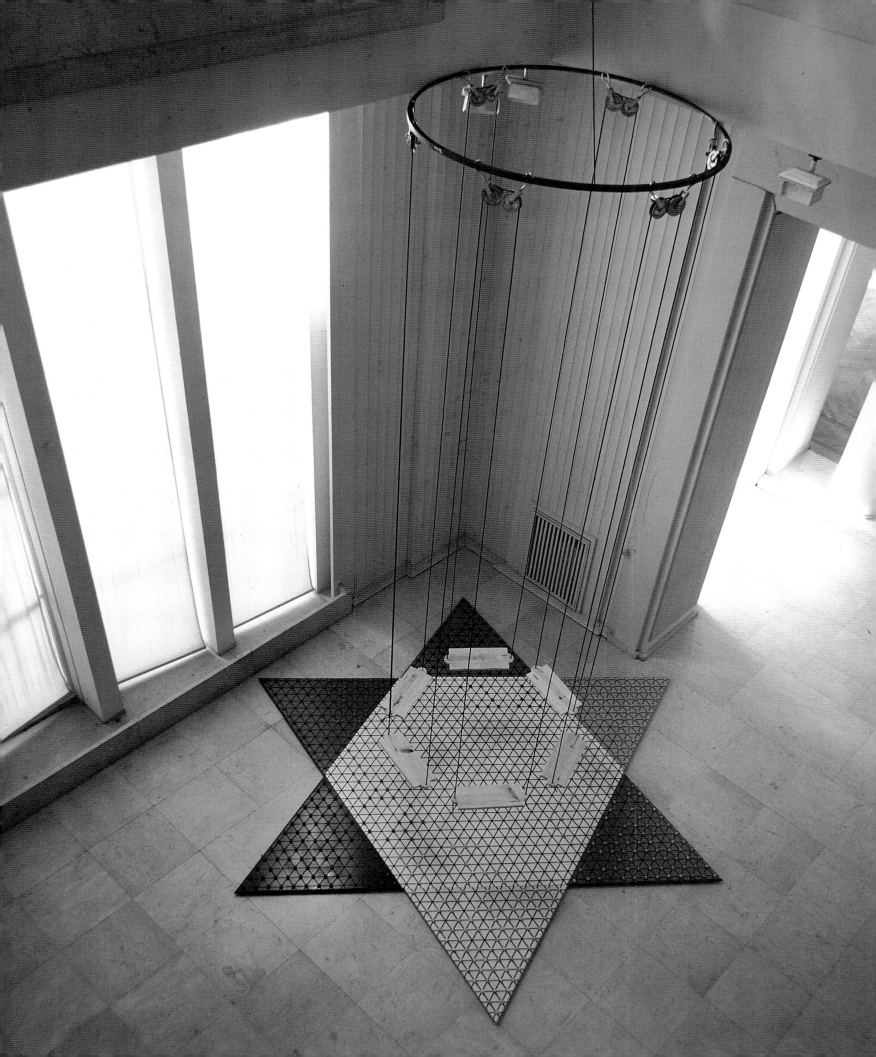

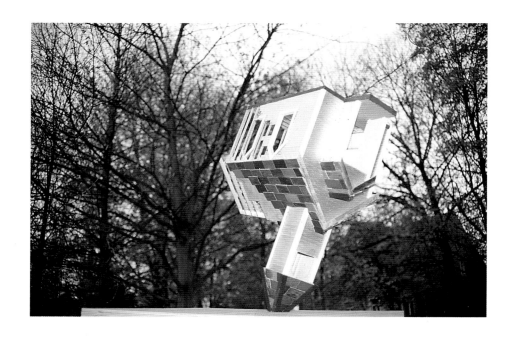

Device to Root Out Evil, 1996

p. 242-243
Double Exposed Kidney Pool, 1997

Drinking Structure with Exposed Kidney Pool, 1997

p. 246-247
Structure Poking it's Eyes Out Resting on Exposed Kidney, 1997

Arriving Structure with Exposed Kidney
Pool, 1997

One of Seven Structural Variations on the
Device Rooting Out Evil, 1997

Retrospective "And the Mind Grew Fingers."
Uiadoski Castle, Warszawa, 1993

p. 254-255
Installation, 1992 (Murder in Hawaiian
Shirts, 1989; Two Objects, 1989)

p. 256-257
Installation, 1993

Doom Room Hanging on a Stroke #2, 1997

Back to Back (Belly to Belly), 1997

p. 264-265
Back to Back (Belly to Belly), 1997

p. 266-267
Buildings Poking their Eyes Out A. One Eye Out B. Two Eyes Out C. Four Eyes Out, 1997

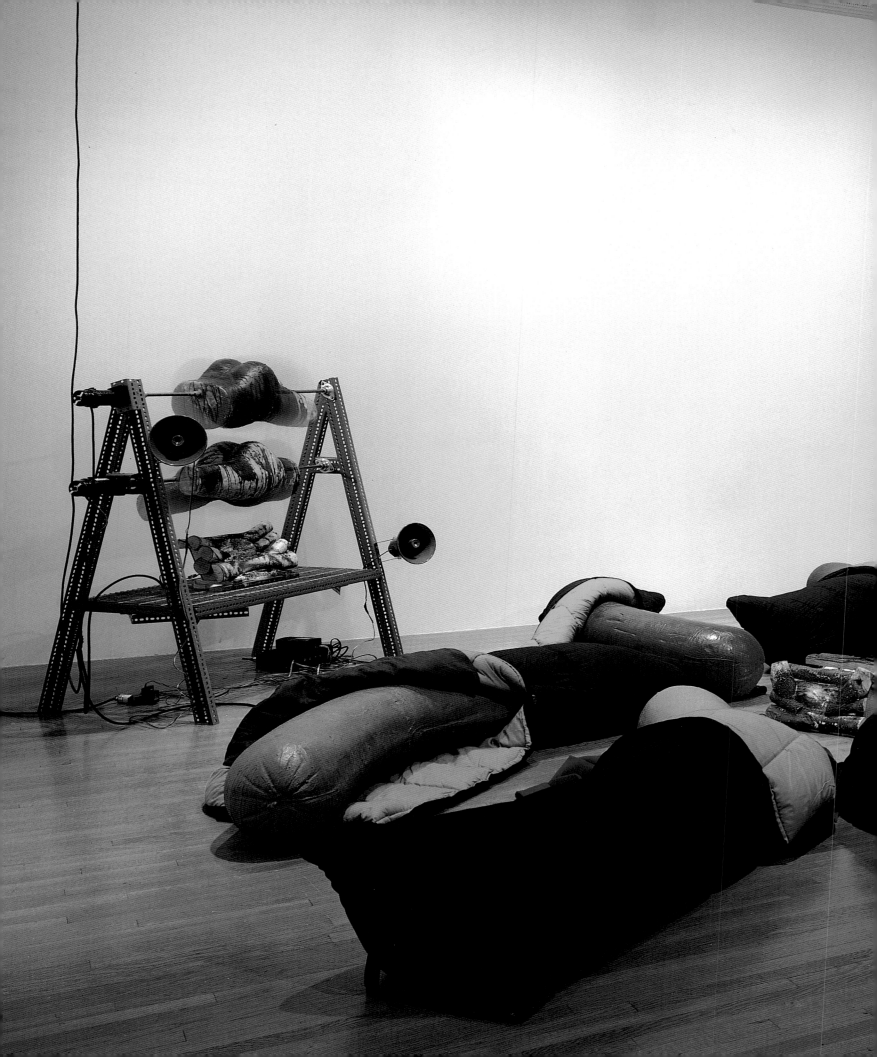

Pear Eating Pumpkin, 1997   *Go Surrounded by Stop, 1997*   p. 270-271
                                                                                                                                                    Installation, 1997

List of Works

The asterisc * marks the exhibited works

Ghost Tantrums. Static Tremors, *1988*

Objects Dream of Flying Terminated by Collision, *1988*

Burnt Rainbow, 1988
Slate, cast resin, cast fiberglass, poured
pigmented fiberglass, cast plaster
6' H x 4' L x 2' D
Photo Ace Contemporary, Los Angeles,
California
see p. 60-61

Dead Beats, 1988
Copper plated steel, rolled steel angle,
perforated steel, silkscreened fiberglass,
silkscreened fabric
3' H x 3' L X 3' D
Private Collection, København, Danmark
Photo Youn Sook Lim, Seoul
see p. 62

Ghost Tantrums. Static Tremors, 1988
Rolled steel, galvanized metal, wood,
silkscreen, fiberglass, electric train, mask,
mirror, casters
3' H x 6.5' L x 12' D
Photo David Sundberg, New York
see p. 273

Image Dissonance. Coffee Cup*, 1988
Steel, spheres, buoys
4' H x 15' L X 15' D
Photo Ace Contemporary, Los Angeles,
California
see p. 64-65

Impersonation Station, 1988
Photo etched aluminum plate, wood, glass,
rolled aluminum, cable, pulleys, concrete,
corten steel, steel rod, topiary trees
25' H x 60' L x 60' D
Olympic Park, Seoul
No Photo

*Objects Dream of Flying Terminated by
Collision*, 1988
Silkscreened fiberglass, wood, silver solder
5' H x 12' L x 6' D
Total Art Museum, Seoul
Photo Walker Hill Art Gallery, Seoul
see p. 273

Second Generation Appliance Spirit #1,
1988
Copper coil, steel, perforated steel, silkscreen,
electric hot plates, cable pulleys, casters
8' H x 2' L x 2' D
No Photo

Soft Collision, *1988*

Stove for High Temperature Expression, *1988*

Steam Forest with Phantom Limbs, *1988*

Second Generation Appliance Spirit #2, 1988
Copper coil, steel, perforated steel,
silkscreen, electric hot plates, cable pulleys,
casters
8' H x 3' L x 3'D
No Photo

Second Generation Appliance Spirit #3,
1988
Copper coil, steel angle, fiberboard,
silkscreen, electric hot plates, cable, pulleys,
casters
8' H x 3' L x 3'D
Photo Youn Sook Lim, Seoul
see p. 58

Second Generation Image -Zebra, 1988
Silkscreened fiberglass over cast fiberglass,
aluminum, wax, wood, pigments
6' H x 7' L x 2' D
Private Collection, Utrecht, Holland
Photo Willoughby Sharp, New York
see p. 59

Second Generation Image. Iron/ Boats, 1988
Cast fiberglass, silkscreen, mirror, wood, red
and blue pigment
6' H x 6' L x 4' D
Private Collection, Varberg, Sverige
No Photo

Second Generation Image. Iron/ Boats, 1988
Cast fiberglass, silkscreen, mirror, wood, blue
and silver pigment
6' H x 6' L x 4' D
Allen Memorial Art Museum, Oberlin, Ohio
No Photo

Second Generation Image. Iron/ Boats, 1988
Marine plywood, silkscreen, mirror, black,
blue and brown pigments, concrete
foundation
8' H x 7' L x 7' D
No Photo

Second Generation Image. Iron/Boats, 1988
Cast fiberglass, silkscreen, red mirror, wood,
red pigment, wood, wax, car
5' H x 2' L x 3' D
Private Collection, New York, New York
Photo David Sundberg, New York
see p. 57

Second Generation Image. Iron/Boats, 1988

Strike*, 1988*

Trumpet*, 1988*

Cast fiberglass, silkscreen, blue mirror, wood, blue pigment, wood, wax, car
5' H X 2' L x 3' D
Private Collection, Belgique
No Photo

Soft Collision, 1988
Wood, foam, colored sponges
2' H x 2' L x 3' D
Photo Willoughby Sharp, New York
see p. 274

Steam Forest with Phantom Limbs, 1988
Pigmented cast fiberglass, electric hot plates, glass
4' H x 4' L x 3' D
Youn Sook Lim, Seoul
see p. 274

Stove for High Temperature Expression, 1988
Cast fiberglass, pigments, electric hot plates, hand blown glass
3' H x 2' L x 1' D
Private Collection, Varberg, Sverige
Photo E. Franck, Knokke le-Zoute, Belgique
see p. 274

Strike, 1988
Bowling pins, bowling balls, fiberglass, silkscreened fiberglass cloth
1' H x 10' L x 9' D
Photo Walker Hill Art Center, Seoul
see p. 275

Third Generation Ghost Toast, 1988
Silkscreened fabric silkscreened fiberglass sheet, perforated metal, wood, pulleys, casters
9' H x 4' L x 3' D
The National Museum of Contemporary Art, Kyungki-do, Korea
No Photo

Thought Bones from Between the Fingers of Fear*, 1988
Colored cast resin, knife blades
1.5' H x 14' L x 2' D
Photo Ace Contemporary, Los Angeles, California
see p. 66

Trumpet, 1988
Steel, copper, electric blower, cable, pulleys, felt

5' H x 8' L x 8' D
The National Museum of Contemporary Art, Kyungki-do, Korea
Photo Youn Sook Lim, Seoul
see p. 275

Two Strikes, 1988
Baseballs bats, softball, silkscreened fiberglass
5' H x 10' L x 4' D
No Photo

Virus, 1988
Marble, aluminum, pigmented cast plaster, scientific clamps
6' H x 6' L x 6' D
The Museum of Fine Arts, Houston, Texas
No Photo

Virus*, 1988
Marble, aluminum, pigmented cast plaster, scientific clamps
7' H x 6' L x 7' D
Photo Ace Contemporary, Los Angeles, California
see p. 63

Whirlpool, 1988
Pigmented cast fiberglass, galvanized metal, water, electric pump, wood, cloth, orange pigments
2' H x 3' L x 3' D
On loan Museum of Contemporary Art, Lake Worth, Florida
No Photo

Whirlpool, 1988
Pigmented cast fiberglass, galvanized metal, water, electric pump, wood, cloth, green and red pigments
2' H x 3' L x 3' D
Photo Walker Hill Art Center, Seoul
see p. 276

Whirlpool, 1988
Pigmented cast fiberglass, galvanized metal, water, electric pump, wood, cloth, blue pigments
2' H x 3' L x 3' D
Private Collection, Varberg, Sverige
No Photo

Wine Glasses Dancing Back to Back, 1988
Steel, cloth buffing disks

275

Whirlpool, *1988*

3' H x 3' L x 2' D
Private Collection, Paris, France
No Photo

Above the Wall of Electrocution, 1989
Steel rack, cable, animal masks, electric
blowers, fabric, electric cord, plugs, timer
8' H x 14' L x 4' D
Pori Art Museum, Pori, Suomi
Photo Ace Contemporary, Los Angeles,
California
see p. 67

*Above the Wall of Electrocution**, 1989
Steel rack, cable, animal masks, electric
blowers, fabric, electric cord, plugs, timer
8' H x 14' L x 4' D
No Photo

*Bad Cells are Comin'**, 1989
Painted brass cymbals, stands, scientific
beakers, turntables, torch, laboratory clamps,
blue ink.
3' H x 8' L x 8' D
Photo David Sundberg, New York
see p. 68-69

Badly Tuned Cow, 1989
Poured pigmented fiberglass, wax, steel,
silkscreened wood, black lights
6' H x 8' L x 8' D
San Jose Museum of Art, San José, California
Photo Ace Contemporary, Los Angeles,
California
see p. 71

Badly Tuned Cow, 1989
Poured pigmented fiberglass, wax, steel,
silkscreened wood, black lights
6' H x 8' L x 8' D
Private Collection, Stockholm, Sverige
No Photo

Buttermilk Run, 1989
Aluminum, steel, perforated steel, electric
motor, rheostat, fishing line, plastic spheres
16' H x 10' L x 10' D
Photo Ivan Dalla Tana, New York
see p. 277

*Buttermilk Run (ceiling) Digestion. Gypsum
Gypsies (floor)*, 1989
Aluminum, steel, perforated steel, electric
motor, rheostat, fishing line, plastic spheres

16' H x 10' L x 10' D
Photo Ivan Dalla Tana, New York
see p. 82-83

Cross Town Tremors, 1989
Drums, wood, speakers, audio tape (drum
beats), tape player
2' H x 7' L x 2' D
Photo Ace Contemporary, Los Angeles,
California
see p. 78

Crystal Tumor, 1989
Wax, fiberglass, torso, steel, crystal
3.2' H x 4.5' L x 25' D
Museum of Modern Art, Antwerp, Belgique
No Photo

Cutting Tool (From the Power Tool Series),
1989
Anodized aluminum, electric drill, electric
cord, electric plugs, hard foam, fiberglass,
mask, wood, mirror, timer
6' H x 2.5' L x 1.5' D
Photo David Sundberg, New York
see p. 90

Digestion #2, 1989
Pigmented fiberglass, gas, wax, rubber hose,
cast resin, regulator, jeweler's torch tips, steel
bolts
2' H x 5' L x 4' D
No Photo

Digestion. Gypsum Gypsies, 1989
Pigmented fiberglass, gas, plaster, wax, rubber
hose, cast resin, regulator, jeweler's torch tips
17' H x 20' L x 20' D
Helsinki City Art Museum, Helsinki, Suomi
Photo Joseph Helman Gallery, New York
see p. 128-129

Digestion. Gypsum Gypsies, 1989
Pigmented fiberglass, gas, wax, rubber hose,
cast resin, regulator, jeweler's torch tips, steel
bolts
5' H x 4' L x 4' D
Norton Collection, Santa Monica, California
No Photo

Digestion, 1989
Pigmented fiberglass, gas, wax, rubber hose,
cast resin, regulator, jeweler's torch tips, steel
bolts

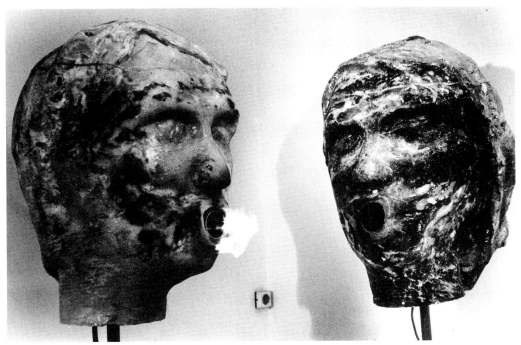

Spinning Dancer - From the Power Tool
Series, *1989*   Wake Collision, *1989*

5' H x 4' L x 2' D
Private Collection, Sweden
Photo David Sundberg, New York
see p. 81

Disco Mattress (From the Power Tool Series), 1989
Steel, diamond plate aluminum, electric saws-alls, electric cord, electric plugs, theatrical spotlights, cloth figures, timer
12' H x 8' L x 8' D
Musée d'art Moderne, Villeneuve d'Ascq, France
Ace Contemporary, Los Angeles, California
see p. 95

Field Guard (From the Power Tool Series), 1989
Steel, diamond plate aluminum, electric drills, electric cord, electric plugs, theatrical spotlights, cloth figures, felt, timer
8' H x 4' L x 4' D
Queensland Art Gallery, Queensland, Australia
No Photo

Five Spinning Dancers (From the Power Tool Series), 1989
Steel, wood, fiberglass, electric drills, electric cord, electric plugs, buffing disk figures,timer
4' H x 5' L x 5' D
The High Museum of Art, Atlanta, Georgia
Photo Ace Contemporary, Los Angeles, California
see p. 94

*Four Spinning Dancers (From the Power Tool Series)**, 1989
Anodized aluminum, electric drills, electric cord, electric plugs, buffing disk figures, wood, mirror, timer
5' H x 6' L x 3' D
Photo Ace Contemporary, Los Angeles, California
see p. 91

Hot Voices, 1989
Cast fiberglass, torch, tanks, copper tubing, regulator
3' H x 12' L x 3' D
Photo David Sundberg, New York
see p. 87

Hot Voices, 1989
Pigmented blue, brown and silver cast

fiberglass, torch, tanks, copper tubing, regulator, steel spring, fiberglass drum
6' H x 8' L x 6' D
Private Collection, Varberg, Sverige
No Photo

Hot Voices, 1989
Tinted cast fiberglass, electric blower, gas torch, steel base, steel tube
6' H x 5' L x 4' D
Photo E. Franck, Knokke le-Zoute, Belgique
see p. 277

Hot Vomit Machine, 1989
Cast fiberglass, steel angle, mirror, donut maker, rubber wheels
5' H x 9.5' L x 2.5' D
Photo Ivan Dalla Tana, New York
see p. 84

Murder in Hawaiian Shirts, 1989
Celastic, silkscreened fluorescent green fabric, plastic toys
3' H x 5' L x 4' D
Museum of Contemporary Art, Honolulu, Hawaii
No Photo

Murder in Hawaiian Shirts, 1989
Celastic, silkscreened beige fabric, plastic toys
3' H x 5' L x 4' D
Photo Ace Contemporary, Los Angeles
see p. 254-255

Shaker with Shakes, 1989
Styrofoam, celastic, metal, salt, pepper
2.5' H x 4' L x 3.3' D
Private Collection, Belgique
Photo Ace Contemporary, Los Angeles, California
see p. 92-93

Slow Clap for Satie, 1989
Acrylic, wood, steel, motors, ficus trees, pots, turntables, vacuum formed masks, tape player, loop recording of piano music
10' H x 20' L x 20' D
Photo Ace Contemporary, Los Angeles, California
see p. 85

Spinning Dancer (From the Power Tool Series), 1989

Anodized aluminum, mirror, electric drills, electric cord, electric plugs, buffing disk figures, timer
5' H x 1.5' L x 2' D
Photo David Sundberg, New York
see p. 278

Spinning Dancers (From the Power Tool Series), 1989
Anodized aluminum, mirror, electric drills, electric cord, electric plugs, buffing disk figures, timer
5' H x 3' L x 2' D
Private Collection, Paris, France
No Photo

Spirit Notes, 1989
Fabric, electric blowers, timers, trumpets, masks, electric cord
5' H x 8' Lx 8' D
Photo Ace Contemporary, Los Angeles, California
see p. 72

Summit to Sadness, 1989
Steel, copper tube, sandblasted wine bottles
16' H x 1' L x 1'D
Photo Ivan Dalla Tana, New York
see p. 88-89

Two Objects, 1989
Silkscreened fabric, wood, foam, piping, motor, aluminum, electric cord, timer
3.3' H x 4.1' L x 3' D
Photo David Sundberg, New York
see p. 73

Two Objects, 1989
Fluorescent fabric, wood, foam, motor, aluminum, electric cord, timer
3.3' H x 4.1' L x 3' D
No Photo

Two Objects, 1989
Paint splattered fabric, wood, foam, motor, aluminum, electric cord, timer
3.3' H x 4.1' L x 3' D
No Photo

Wake Collision, 1989
Cast pigmented foam, sailboats, acrylic, steel
1.5 D 10' H x 5' L x 5' D
Photo David Sundberg, New York
see p. 278

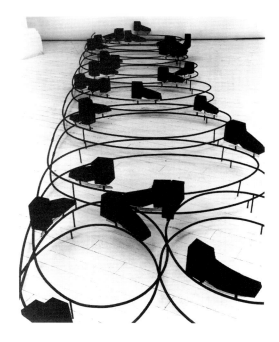

Woman with Halo, 1989
Wood, colored chalk, electric train set
1.5' H x 7' L x 3' D
Photo Liverpool Gallery, Brussel, Belgique
see p. 76-77

Black Pool*, 1990
Wood, steel, aluminum rod, billiard balls,
bowling balls, black pipe, felt
6' H x 8' L x 4' D
Centro de Arte Reina Sofia, Madrid, España
Photo David Sundberg, New York
see p. 79

Blackware, 1990
Hand blown, scientific beakers, laboratory
clamps, steel
8' H x 14' Lx 14' D
No Photo

Figure Skating, 1990
Wood, copper, acid treated aluminum
1' H x 18' L x 4.5' D
Private Collection, Andorra
No Photo

Figure Skating*, 1990
Wood, copper, acid treated aluminum
5' H x 36' L x 7' D
Photo Ace Contemporary, Los Angeles,
California
see p. 109

Photo David Sundberg, New York
see p. 280

Functioning Faces, 1990
Ceramic urinals, paint, steel, electric pump
(behind wall), infrared motion detector
9' H x 21' L x 1.1' D
Marcel Fleiss, Paris, France
Photo David Sundberg, New York
see p. 74-75

Hey Joe, 1990
Wood, cast epoxy, steel, acrylic, soundtrack,
turntable, speakers
12' H x 9' L x 9' D
No Photo

Jack-Offs, 1990
Pigmented cast epoxy
4' H x 18' L x 18' D
No Photo

Kiss, 1990
Steel with baked enamel, diamond plate,
rolled plate, casters, water, masks electric
fans, turntable
12' H x 10' L x 6' D
Photo Ace Contemporary, Los Angeles,
California
see p. 112-113

Kissing Racks, 1990
Aluminum, vacuum formed plastic, cord,
electric turntables
9' H x 8' L x 4' D
Helsinki City Art Museum, Helsinki, Suomi
Photo Ace Contemporary, Los Angeles, California
see p. 119

Revolving Kissing Racks, 1990
Metal bottle racks, colored cast resin, cord,
electric turntable
3' H x 6' L x 3' D
F.R.A.C., Clermont Ferrand, France
No Photo

Revolving Kissing Racks, 1990
Metal bottle racks, vacuum formed plastic,
cord, electric turntable
3' H x 6' L x 3'D
Private Collection, France
No Photo

Stacked Friends, 1990
Cast fiberglass, mannequin, dolls, paint
4.5' H x 1.5' L x 3' D
No Photo

*Toe to Heel. Woman Trapped in a Man's
Body*, 1990
Aluminum, rod, wire mesh, motorized
turntable, wax figure
14' H x 8' L x 4' D
Kroller-Muller Museum, Otterlo, Holland
Photo Ace Contemporary, Los Angeles,
California
see p. 115

Untitled Installation*, 1990
Hard foam, beeswax, rubber hose, cast resin,
gas, regulator, jeweler's torch tips, black tar,
poured pigmented fiberglass
8' H x 12' L x 12' D
No Photo

Untitled Wall Piece, 1990

Crystal Waste, *1991*

Hard foam, beeswax, rubber hose, cast resin,
gas, regulator, jeweler's torch tips
8' H x 7' L x 3' D
Collection Broska, Mainz, Deutschland
Photo David Sundberg, New York
see p. 116

Untitled Wall Piece, 1990
Hard foam, beeswax, rubber hose, cast resin,
gas, regulator, jeweler's torch tips, orange
pigments
8' H x 7' L x 3' D
Private Collection, France
No Photo

*Vibrating Figures (From the Power Tool
Series)*, 1990
Steel, electric sanders, electric cord, electric
plugs, cloth figures, timer
12' H x 6' L x 6' D
Photo Weatherspoon Art Gallery, Greensboro,
North Carolina
see p. 107

Aw-ful Waffle, 1991
Vacuum formed plastic, sheet rock, wood,
speakers, rolled steel, audio track, amplifier
16' H x 50' L x 8' D
Photo David Sundberg, New York
see p. 96-97

Between Drinks, 1991
Confetti, cast fiberglass
2' H x 30' L x 30' D
Fundaçao de Serralves, Oporto, Portugal
No Photo

Between Drinks (floor) Double Headed
Woman with Floating Hearts (wall)*, 1991
Confetti, cast fiberglass, Heated bottles,
shaped sponges, colored water, ink, glass
4' H x 30' L x 30' D
Photo David Sundberg, New York
see p. 104

Black, 1991
Pigmented cast fiberglass, audio track, amplifier
4.5' H x 40' L x 40' D
The Art Museum of Florida, Atlantic
University, Miami, Florida
Photo Ace Contemporary, Los Angeles
see p. 120-121

Combined Expressions, 1991

Galvanized steel
10' H x 10' L x 10' D
Cedarhurst Sculpture Park, Mount Vernon,
Illinois
Photo Ace Contemporary, Los Angeles,
California
see p. 117

Crystal Waste, 1991
Cast fiberglass, steel, formed acrylic
14' H x 14' L x 2'D
No Photo

Crystal Waste*, 1991
Tinted cast fiberglass, steel, rocks
14' H x 14' L x 2' D
Photo David Sundberg, New York
see p. 281

*Double Headed Woman with Floating
Hearts*, 1991
Heated bottles, shaped sponges, colored
water, ink, glass
5' H x 16' L x 1' D
Photo Ace Contemporary, Los Angeles,
California
see p. 105

Flaming Moose, 1991
Poured pigmented fiberglass, cast resin,
copper tube, jeweler's tips, gas, rubber hose,
regulator
10' H x 4' L x 4' D
Fundaçao de Serralves, Oporto, Portugal
Photo David Sundberg, New York
see p. 282

Flaming Moose, 1991
Wax, cast resin, copper tube, jeweler's tips,
gas, rubber hose, regulator
10' H x 4' L x 4' D
Skulpturen Museum Glaskasten Marl, Marl,
Deutschland
No Photo

Kiss, 1991
Rolled steel channel, expanded steel, white
birds, black birds, inner tubes
16' H x 20' L x 2.4' D
Musée d'art Moderne, Villeneuve d'Ascq,
France
Photo David Sundberg, New York
see p. 98-99

Rag Head, 1991

Flaming Moose, *1991*

Cast fiberglass, plastic sheet, wallpaper, steel, electric motors, tracks, cable, plastic pipe, timers
8' H x 22' L x 22' D
Photo David Sundberg, New York
see p. 283

Searchburst, 1991
Rolled steel angle, perforated steel, flashing lights, cable
20' H x 15' L x 5' D
Photo David Sundberg, New York
see p. 100

Slave Cactus, 1991
Sheet rock, oars, oar locks, wood
1' H x 40' L x 40' D
Norton Gallery of Art, West Palm Beach, Florida
Photo David Sundberg, New York
see p. 108

Stab, 1991
Rolled steel angle, steel plate, vacuum formed colored plastic
4.5' H x 40' L x 30' D
Ace Contemporary, Los Angeles, California
see p. 102-103

Vibrating Dolls (From the Power Tool Series), 1991
Steel, diamond plate aluminum, electric saws-alls, electric cord, electric plugs, theatrical spotlights, cloth figures, timer
3.5' H x 6.25' L x 3' D
No Photo

Black Dog in Cage, 1992
Wood, press board, hard foam, acrylic, animal form, soundtrack (barking dog) amplifier, speakers
9.3' H x 8. 3' L x 6' D
Centro de Arte Reina Sofia, Madrid, España
Photo Joseph Helman Gallery, New York
see p. 127

*Gut Birthdays**, 1992
Steel, electric cord, clamps, wood, wet suits, light fixtures, neon, weights, cable
10' H x 20' L x 12' D
Photo Joseph Helman Gallery, New York
see p. 123

Long Distance Anger, 1992

Rubber hose, garden hose, foam, electrical clamps
8' H x 18' L x 18' D
Musée d'art Contemporain et Moderne, Genève, Suisse
Photo Haines Gallery, San Francisco, California
see p. 130

*Lungs with Brushes Heart with Paper Liver with Pencils**, 1992
Brushes, paper, pencils, wood, hard foam, paint, glitter, electric turntables, cord
7' H x 40' L x 20' D
Photo Joseph Helman Gallery, New York
see p. 136-137

Tempest in a Teacup, 1992
Rolled steel tube, perforated steel, sandblasted glass
20' H x 29' L x 29' D
Principat d'Andorra, Andorra
Photo J.M. Ubach, Andorra
see p. 131

Upper Cut, 1992
Wood, press board, hard foam, art books
5.1' H x 6' L x 5.7' D
The Museum of Contemporary Art, Honolulu, Hawaii
Photo Joseph Helman Gallery, New York
see p. 124-125

*Upper Cut**, 1992
Wood, press board, hard foam, art books
3' H x 3' L x 3' D
Photo Cheryl Haines Gallery, San Francisco, California
see p. 283

Wal-nuts, 1992
Vacuum formed plastic, two video tapes with audio, two video monitors
14' H x 14' L x 4' D
track 1: "wa..wa..wa..wa..wall..wall......"
track 2: "nu...nu...nu...nuts...nu..."
Photo Joseph Helman Gallery, New York
see p. 135

Beasts from Canal Street, 1993
Foam, plastic, fruits, animals, cord, steel, galvanized hosing, celastic
9' H x 30' L x 16' D
Photo Weatherspoon Art Gallery, Greensboro,

North Carolina
see p. 153

Bed Piece*, 1993
Folding beds, casters, steel frame, steel
channel, springs, fiberglass masks
4' H x 12' L x 12' D
Photo Weatherspoon Art Gallery, Greensboro,
North Carolina
see p. 150-151

Blue Tattoo, 1993
Sewn silkscreened fabric, border light,
projector, spotlight, motorized bull,
galvanized pan, camera, kettles, hot plates,
hosing, timer
16' H x 25' L x 25' D
Photo Joseph Helman Gallery, New York
see p. 170-171

Color Wars, 1993
Clothe, cotton, shredded cellophane, cast
animal's jaws
1' H x 8' L x 8' D
No Photo

Divorce, 1993
Tinted cast fiberglass
2' H x 18' L x 3' D
A. Indini, Roma
see p. 146-147

Galloping through the Wheat*, 1993
Foam rubber, patinaed cast bronze, knives
3' H x 10' L x 5' D
Photo Joseph Helman Gallery, New York
see p. 142-143

Gathering, 1993
Steel, formed plaster, cast beeswax, candle
wicks
3' H x 8' L x 3' D
Collection Broska, Mainz, Deutschland
A. Indini, Roma
see p. 145

Gathering*, 1993
Steel, formed plaster, cast beeswax, candle
wicks
3' H x 8' L x 3' D
No Photo

Hair Piece from Hell, 1993
Steel, wire mesh, brushes

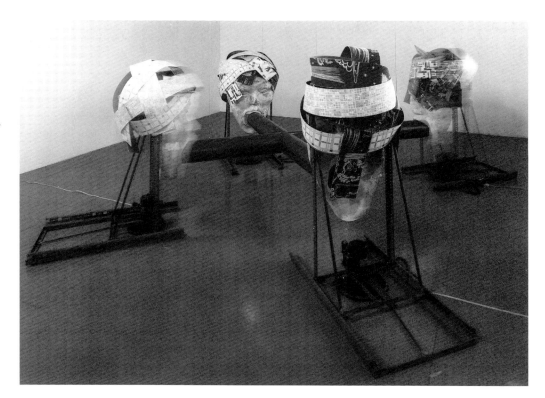

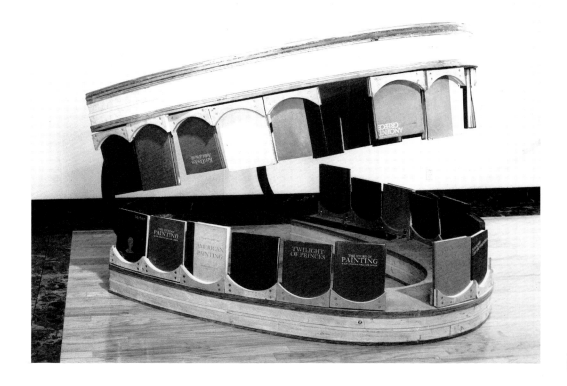

Spinning Shark, *1994*

4' H x 4' L x 4' D
No Photo

Hair Piece from Hell, 1993
Steel, wire mesh, colored mop yarn
3' H x 4.1' L x 3' D
No Photo

Hair Piece from Hell, 1993
Steel, wire mesh, buffing disks
3' H x 4.1' L x
3.3' D
No Photo

Hair Piece from Hell, 1993
Steel, wire mesh, copper scrubbing pads
3' H x 4.1' L x 3.3' D
No Photo

Hair Piece from Hell, 1993
Steel, wire mesh, sanding disks
3' H x 4.1' L x 3.3' D
No Photo

Heavy Dog Kiss, 1993
Pigmented cast fiberglass, rocks, brick, bolts
8' H x 4' L x 4' D
Private Collection, Napoli
Photo Joseph Helman Gallery, New York
see p. 140

Heavy Dog Kiss, 1993
Pigmented cast fiberglass, cement blocks,
bowling balls, buoys, rocks, bolts
8' H x 4' L x 4' D
Allen Memorial Art Gallery, Oberlin, Ohio
No Photo

Heavy Dog Kiss*, 1993
Pigmented cast fiberglass, cement blocks,
rocks, plants, cast plaster, bolts
8' H x 4' L x 4' D
No Photo

Kick, 1993
Steel rod, mesh, rope lighting, packing pellets
8' H x 11' L x 9' D
Photo Weatherspoon Art Gallery, Greensboro,
North Carolina
see p. 149

Starmen*, 1993
Rubber tires, water, planters, galvanized
pans, underwater strobe lighting,
transformers
1' H x 27' L x 27' D

Photo Weatherspoon Art Gallery, Greensboro, North Carolina
see p. 148

Swarm, 1993
Cast silver, silver wire
6' H x 15' L x 3' D
No Photo

Sweet Wars, 1993
Sewn plastic, masks, cast chocolate, jellybeans
1' H x 8' L x 8' D
No Photo

Think Tanks, 1993
Plastic coated cloth, fabric, paint, train track, engines, transformers, wood
5' H x 13' L x 6.5' D
Photo Joseph Helman Gallery, New York
see p. 138-139

Untitled, 1993
Chicken wire, plaster, pigmented cast plaster
6' H x 14' L x 13' D
Photo Joseph Helman Gallery, New York
see p. 168

Sweet Wars, 1993
Cast chocolate, sugar cubes
1' H x 10' L x 10' D
Photo A. Indini, Roma
see p. 144

Untitled Drum Accompaniment*, 1993
Cast fiberglass, drum, electric motor, foot petal, electric cord
1.5' H x 4' L x 1.5' D
Photo Galerie Albrecht, München , Deutschland
see p. 172

Village around Piss Lake, 1993
Cardboard, colored beeswax, galvanized pan, electric strobe light, cast acrylic
1.5' H x 3' L x 3' D
No Photo

Woman with Cubist Tendencies*, 1993
Hard foam, plaster, mannequin, plastic, cloth, electric blower
8' H x 4' L x 4' D
Photo Galerie Albrecht, München, Deutschland
see p. 181

Bat Flying Out of a Cat's Ear, 1994
Welded copper wire, plaster, lathe, wood, pigments
2' H x 3' L x 3' D
No Photo

Battered Tears, 1994
Hard foam, colored resin, two video tapes with audio, two video monitors, electric cord, wood
14' H x 14' L x 6' D
Museum van Hedendaagse Kunst, Gent, Belgique
Photo Joseph Helman Gallery, New York
see p. 156-157

Circle Puppets, 1994
Colored acrylic, two video tapes with audio, two video monitors, electric cord, wood, aluminum, rubber, hose, clamps
12' H x 12' L x 12' D
Centro de Arte Reina Sofia, Madrid, España
Photo Joseph Helman Gallery, New York
see p. 158

Clothed Organ*, 1994
Steel, mesh, hard foam, pigment, rubber tubing
7' H x 7' L x 4' D
Photo Joseph Helman Gallery, New York
see p. 155

Finger Churches*, 1994
Carved hard foam, beeswax
4' H x 4' L x 4' D
Photo Joseph Helman Gallery, New York
see p. 169

Hot Tattoos*, 1994
Steel, steel rod, wire mesh, polyvinyl tube, electric fire logs, turntable, silkscreen.
16' H x 9' L x 9' D
Photo Joseph Helman Gallery, New York
see p. 159

Incident at Stutter Pond, 1994
Wood, corrugated fiberglass, asphalt shingle, truck, wire mesh, fiberglass, pigment, rubber tires, acrylic, boat, rope lighting, vacuum formed letter
8' H x 50' L x 40' D
Photo M. Lerouge, Villeneuve d'ascq, France
see p. 174-179

Iron/Cactus, 1994
Irons, electric cord, electric plugs, steel, cacti, clay pots, soil, gravel
6' H x 8' L x 1' D
Photo Joseph Helman Gallery, New York
see p. 154

Searchburst Complex, 1994
Steel rod, steel mesh, auto reflectors, bolts, steel angle, rope lighting
8' H x 30' L x 40' D
University of Hartford, West Hartford, Connecticut
No Photo

Spinning Shark*, 1994
Tinted cast fiberglass, steel, electric cord, motor, timer
9' H x 7' L x 6' D
Photo Joseph Helman Gallery, New York
see p. 167

Photo Butler Art Institute, Youngstown, Ohio
see p. 284

Stutter Pen*, 1994
Steel angle, steel rod, motors, spotlights, acrylic, electric cord, electric plugs, cable, timers
12' H x 18' L x 16' D
Photo Joseph Helman Gallery, New York
see p. 160-161

The Last Dance, 1994
Hard foam, nails, fiberglass, pigment, record player, record, cable, timer
10' H x 7' L x 7' D
Photo Joseph Helman Gallery, New York
see p. 164-165

The Last Dance Installation, 1994
Hard foam, nails, fiberglass, pigment, radios, record player, record, cable, electric cord, drum, motor, foot petal, stage lighting, acrylic, steel, timers
18' H x 40' L x 40' D
Photo The Children's Museum, San Diego, California
see p. 162

Wolf Trucks: Mobile Land Activators*, 1994
Cardboard, wax, resin, masks, electric lights, electric cord, timers
2' H x 13' L x 7' D
Photo Joseph Helman Gallery, New York
see p. 180

Bat Flying Out of a Cat's Ear, 1994-97
Welded steel tube, perforated steel, expanded
steel, copper, fiberglass, plaster, lathe, wood,
pigments, earth
20' H x 8' L x 8' D
Work in Progress, Comune du Lamentin,
Guadalupe
No Photo

Bad, 1995
Wood, hard foam, plaster, pigments, wax, cast
beeswax
1' H x 3' L x 3' D
No Photo

Birthing Animal, 1995
Copper wire, electric lights, cast animal's
jaws
1' H x 4' L x 4' D
Photo Galerie Berndt, Köln, Deutschland
see p. 287

Black Ball*, 1995
Clothe netting, fabric, steel, mask, cable,
bowling ball
8' H x 9' L x 4' D
Photo Kunstbunker, München, Deutschland
see p. 190-191

Black Spaghetti*, 1995
Rubber hose, sponge, hard foam, plaster,
mannequin, wood, acrylic
4' H x 20' L x 20' D
No Photo

Campfire*, 1995
Wood, wax, pigment, steel wire
1' H x 3' L x 3' D
Photo Drew Cliness, New York
see p. 193

Chair/Pool, 1995
Steel rod, wire mesh, plaster, wooden base,
corrugated plastic
2.5' H x 3' L x 3' D
Photo Drew Cliness, New York
see p. 192

Color Mix, 1995
Rolled steel pipe, steel mesh, wood, poured
powdered pigments
1' H x 4' L x 3' D
Photo Drew Cliness, New York
see p. 194

Earmuffs*, 1995
Rolled steel, sponge
4' H x 4' L x 4'D
No Photo

Earmuffs, 1995
Rolled steel, steel mesh, colored cotton balls
4' H x 4' L x 4' D
Raccolta dei Campiani, Brescia
Photo Ierimonti Gallery, Milano
see p. 189

Enclosures for Blue and Red Gardens, 1995
Wood, steel, perforated steel, trees
2' H x 2' L x 2' D
No Photo

Flower Bed, 1995
Wood, wax, powdered pigment
5' H x 3' L x 4' D
No Photo

*Four Chimneys with Ground Based Sodium
Vapor Lights*, 1995
Brick, cement, hedges, underground light,
rotating tree
2' H x 3' L x 3' D
Tweed Museum of Art, Duluth, Minnesota
Photo Drew Cliness, New York
see p. 197

Fruit Dick, 1995
Pigmented fiberglass over plastic fruits, steel
support
6' H x 3' L x 8' D
No Photo

Grey, 1995
Wood, wax, hard foam, powdered pigment
1' H x 3' L x 3' D
B-L-A-C-K- W-H-I-T-E
No Photo

Incubator with Spinning Trees, 1995
Galvanized fencing, steel mesh, aluminum
siding, light poles, galvanized stacks
3' H x 3' L x 3' D
Tweed Museum of Art, Duluth,
Minnesota
Photo Drew Cliness, New York
see p. 195

Kidney Shaped Pool (On it's Side)*, 1995
Cast pigmented resin, wood, wax, pigments

1' H x 1' L x 1' D
No Photo

Land Net*, 1995
Shaped hedges, wood, foam, pigment
8' H x 4' L x 2.6' D
Photo Drew Cliness, New York
see p. 202

Love/Hate, 1995
Carved hard foam, tinted fiberglass, masks,
trumpet, strobe light, speakers, audio tape
5' H x 7' L x 7' D
soundtrack: (repeating)
"Lori...Olive...Violet...Ellen...Harry....Alice...Terry.....Elmer..."
Private Collection, Suisse
Photo Galerie van der Spek, Amsterdam,
Holland
see p. 183

Makin' Cunts, 1995
Cut wooden clogs, pigments
1' H x 10' L x 6' D
No Photo

*Outdoor Proposal with Concrete Curtains,
Angled Bleachers, Hedges with Spinning
Trees*, 1995
Steel, concrete, wood, hedges, pigment
2.6' H x 3.3' L x 2.6' D
Photo Tweed Museum of Art, Duluth,
Minnesota
see p. 198

Project for a Lake*, 1995
Wood, acrylic, asphalt shingle, canvas,
concrete, stone, hard foam, pigment
1' H x 8' L x 4' D
Photo Drew Cliness, New York
see p. 196

Rabbit Factory, 1995
Steel, expanded steel, colored aluminum,
pigmented cast fiberglass, acrylic, concrete
14' H x 35' L x 35' D
Ballerup Kommune, Ballerup, Danmark
Photo Planet/Ryberg, København, Danmark
see p. 210-211

Rabbit Factory, 1995
Cast resin, plaster, galvanized steel, wood,
fiberglass, aluminum, perforated steel,
pigment
2' H x 4' L x 3' D

Birthing Animal, *1995*

Photo Drew Cliness, New York
see p. 207

Secret Eyes, 1995
Wood, hard foam, wax, pigments
1' H x 5' L x 4' D
No Photo

Silver Bullets, 1995
Wood, hard foam, metal, wax, pigments
1' H x 3' L x 4' D
No Photo

Silver Tears, 1995
Galvanized steel, perforated steel, steel angle,
wood, fiberglass, hard foam, cast fiberglass,
pigment, wire, electric fans, cotton, vacuum
cleaners, air blowers, submersible pump
12' H x 30' L x 30' D
Photo Jeff Frey and Associates, Duluth, Minnesota
see p. 173

Slime Charms, 1995
Cast aluminum, cable
8' H x 9' L x 1'D
No Photo

Submerged Faces, 1995
Cast fiberglass, wood, pigment, acrylic
2' H x 4' L x 2' D
Photo Tweed Museum of Art, Duluth, Minnesota
see p. 200-201

Suburban Drift, 1995
Concrete, tile, canvas, wood, acrylic, pigment
1' H x 4.1' L x 4' D
Photo Drew Cliness, New York
see p. 204-205

T- House,* 1995
Wood, hard foam, pigments, plaster, screening
3' H x 2' L x 2' D
No Photo

The Old in and Out, 1995
Wood, cheesecloth, pigmented fiberglass
resin, train track, engines, colored paper
tunnels
1' H x 7' L x 7' D
Photo Galerie van der Spek, Amsterdam,
Holland
see p. 186-187

Tulip Run-a Jogging Course, 1995

Cement, wood, wax, pigment
8' H x 3.6' L x 3' D
Photo Drew Cliness, New York
see p. 203

Vertical Pool, 1995
Tile, wood, pigments, fiberglass, pigment
2' H x 3' L x 3' D
Photo Drew Cliness, New York
see p. 199

Windmill*, 1995
Wood, electric motor, lace, vacuum formed
letters
 8' H x 8' L X 2' D
Photo Liz Leggett, New York
see p. 184-185

A Ring for Every Finger*, 1996
Carved hard foam, fiberglass, rubber tires,
electric lights, glass
6' H x 10' L x 10' D
Photo Antonio Pinto, Oporto, Portugal
see p. 232-233

Bear Factory #1*, 1996
Wood, wax, pigments, triangular board,
galvanized steel, aluminum, cast beeswax
1' H x 1.5' L x 1.5' D
No Photo

Bear Factory #2, 1996
Wood, wax, pigments, octangular board,
galvanized steel, aluminum
1' H x 1.5' L x 1.5' D
No Photo

Blood Breathe*, 1996
Carved hard foam, galvanized steel grating,
stainless steel, electric hot plates, water,
pigment, timer
4' H x 8' L x 5m D
Photo Drew Cliness, New York
see p. 235

Blushing Machine, 1996
Rolled steel pipe, electric lights, red bulbs,
cast fiberglass, electric dimmer control
3' H x 7' L x 7' D
Galeries Contemporaines, Musée de
Marseille, Marseille, France
No Photo

Blushing Machine*, 1996

Steel tube, electric lights, red bulbs, cast
fiberglass, lawn roller, electric dimmer control
5' H x 12' L x 4' D
Photo Antonio Pinto, Oporto, Portugal
see p. 229

Candelabra*, 1996
Galvanized cans, steel woks, stainless steel
pots, steel plate, rolled steel tube, cast
beeswax, electric cord, electric pianos,
electric fixtures
14' H x 10' L x 3' D
Photo Antonio Pinto, Oporto, Portugal
see p. 239

Chair/Pool, 1996
Rolled steel pipe, steel mesh, concrete, lathe,
electric pumps
18' H x 18' L x 27' D
Europos Parkas, Vilnius, Lietuvà
Photo Europos Parkas, Vilnius, Lietuvà
see p. 208-209

Church*, 1996
Wood, wax, pigments, galvanized steel,
aluminum
1' H x 1' L x 1' D
No Photo

Collision Catalyst, 1996
Wood, wax, hard foam, pigments
1' H x 1' L x 1' D
No Photo

Device to Root Out Evil, 1996
Wood, aluminum, pigment, concrete
3.3' H x 3' L x 3' D
Photo Henry Rich, New York
see p. 241

Elephant Factory, 1996
Wood, wax, pigments, galvanized steel,
aluminum, cast beeswax
1' H x 1' L x 1' D
No Photo

Engagement, 1996
Rolled steel, wood, tinted clear and green cast
resin, paint, light
2.8' H x 2.3' L x 2.3' D
Photo Henry Rich, New York
see p. 220

Engagement, 1996

Rolled steel, wood, tinted red and blue cast
resin, paint, light
2.8' H x 2.3' L x 2.3' D
Photo Henry Rich, New York
see p. 221

Engagement*, 1996
Rolled steel, wood, tinted white and blue cast
resin, paint, light
2.8' H x 2.3' L x 2.3' D
No Photo

Fast Exit*, 1996
Wood, pigmented cast beeswax
3' H x 3' L x 6' D
Photo Städtische Galerie Nordhorn, Deutschland
see p. 237

Four Cornered Murder*, 1996
Steel, wood, yarn
Photo Antonio Pinto, Oporto, Portugal
see p. 222-223

Half Ass, 1996
Welded curved steel rod, ceramic pots, soil,
plants
9' H x 5' L x 7' D
No Photo

Lamp Dog, 1996
Welded curved steel rod, lamps, electrical
cord, circular bread loaves
16' H x 6.5m L x 16' D
No Photo

Pig Factory, 1996
Wood, gravel, expanded metal, steel rod, cast
beeswax, pigment
2' H x 2' L x 2' D
Photo Cliness, New York
see p. 213

Products from the Snowman Factory, 1996
Wood, metal, fiberglass, pigment
5' H x 12' L x 10' D
Photo Antonio Pinto, Oporto, Portugal
see p. 217

Proposal for Building Complex, 1996
Hard foam, pigmented cast acrylic
5' H x 5' Lx 3' D
No Photo

Ski Houses*, 1996

Aluminum, wood, wax, pigment, plaster, acrylic
5' H x 4' W x 2' D
Photo Antonio Pinto, Oporto, Portugal
see p. 215

Snowman Factory*, 1996
Aluminum, wood, pigment, acrylic, perforated steel
2' H x 5' L x 4' D
Photo Drew Cliness, New York
see p. 218-219

Tar Roses, 1996
Tinted cast fiberglass, concrete
6' H x 45' L x 45' D
Photo Antonio Pinto, Oporto, Portugal
see p. 227

Topiary Piece*, 1996
Welded curved steel rod, ceramic pots, soil, plants
7' H x 9' L x 9' D
Photo Antonio Pinto, Oporto, Portugal
see p. 224-225

Tornado Houses*, 1996
Aluminum, wood, wax, pigment, plaster, acrylic
5' H x 3' L x 2'
Foto Antonio Pinto, Oporto, Portugal
see p. 214

Turtle Factory, 1996
Wood, wax, pigments, galvanized steel, aluminum, cast beeswax
1' H x 1.5' L x 1.5' D
No Photo

Untitled, 1996
Painted wood, glass marbles, rope, wood, rolled steel, pulleys
15' H x 12' L x 12' D
Photo Antonio Pinto, Oporto, Portugal
see p. 231

Vertical Pool*, 1996
Tile, wood, pigments, fiberglass, pigment
1' H x 1' L x 1' D
No Photo

Arriving Structure with Exposed Kidney Pool, 1997
Welded curved copper wire, tinted cast resin
3' H x 3' L x 5' D
Photo Henry Rich, New York
see p. 248-249

Back to Back (Belly to Belly)*, 1997
Perforated steel angle, galvanized grating, fiberglass, wax, torso, electric motor, audio tape
4.5' H x 5' L x 3' D
Photo Erma Estwick, New York
see p. 263

Buildings Poking their Eyes Out A. One Eye Out B. Two Eyes Out C. Four Eyes Out*, 1997
Corrugated fiberglass, rolled galvanized metal, wax, fiberboard, pigments
2' H x 16' L x 5' D
Photo Erma Estwick, New York
see p. 266-267

Device to Root out Evil*, 1997
Structural iron, diamond pattern perforated iron, anodized aluminum, glass, red glass shingles, rubber, electric light, concrete foundations
22' H x 9' L x 18' D
The Denver Art Museum, Promised Gift of Ginny Williams, Courtesy Joseph Helman Gallery
No Photo

Doom Room Hanging on a Stroke #1, 1997
Plaster with wax, sheet rock, rubber strap, steel
6.5' H x 10' L x 3.3' D
Photo Erma Estwick, New York
see p. 259

Doom Room Hanging on a Stroke #2*, 1997
Plaster with wax, sheet rock, rubber strap, steel
5' H x 11' L x 3.7' D
Photo Erma Estwick, New York
see p. 258

Double Exposed Kidney Pool, 1997
Tinted cast resin
1' H x 3' L x 2' D
Photo Henry Rich, New York
see p. 242-243

Drinking Structure with Exposed Kidney Pool, 1997

Corrugated fiberglass, wood, expanded steel, tinted cast resin
3' H x 4' L x 3' D
Photo Henry Rich, New York
see p. 244-245

Go Surrounded by Stop*, 1997
Cast fiberglass, steel, electric fixtures, light bulbs, lighting controller, electric wire
12' H x 40' L x 40' D
Photo Erma Estwick, New York
see p. 269

One of Seven Structural Variations on the Device Rooting Out Evil, 1997
Wood, aluminum paint, tinted cast resin
4' H x 3' L x 3' D
Photo Henry Rich, New York
see p. 251

Pear Eating Pumpkin*, 1997
Steel, pigmented cast fiberglass, bolts, electric light
9' H x 4' L x 5' D
Photo Erma Estwick, New York
see p. 268

Sleeping Dogs*, 1997
Pigmented cast fiberglass, pigmented wax, sleeping bags, blankets
2' H x 6.5' L x 6.5' D
Photo Erma Estwick, New York
see p. 260-261

Structure Poking it's Eyes Out Resting on Exposed Kidney, 1997
Corrugated fiberglass, wood, expanded steel, tinted cast resin
4' H x 4' L x 4' D
Photo Henry Rich, New York
see p. 246-247

Exhibitions

Solo exhibitions
1968
John Gibson Gallery, New York, New York, U.S.A.

1969
John Gibson Gallery, "Below Zero Projects," New York, New York, U.S.A.
Galerie Yvon Lambert, Paris
Françoise Lambert, Milano

1970
Reese Palley, San Francisco, California, U.S.A.
John Gibson Gallery, New York, New York, U.S.A.
Pennsylvania Art Museum, Erie, Pennsylvania, U.S.A.
Lia Rumma, Napoli
Crossman Gallery, Wisconsin State University, Whitewater, Wisconsin, U.S.A.

1971
Galerie Yvon Lambert, Paris
Françoise Lambert, Milano
Harcus Krakow Gallery, Boston, Massachusetts, U.S.A.
Gallery 20, Amsterdam

1972
Sonnabend Gallery, New York, New York, U.S.A.
Nova Scotia College of Art and Design, Halifax, Nova Scotia, Canada
Mathais Felds, Paris
Tate Gallery, London
L'Attico, Roma
Gallery D, Brussel

1973
Sonnabend Gallery, Paris
Sonnabend Gallery, New York, New York, U.S.A.
Galleria Forma, Genova
Gallery D, Brussel
Gallery Mayor, London
Museum of Contemporary Art, San Francisco, California, U.S.A.
Rivkin Gallery, Washington, D.C., U.S.A.

1974
Stedelijk Museum, Amsterdam
John Gibson Gallery, New York, New York, U.S.A.
Oppenheim Studio, Köln
Gallery D, Brussel
Paolo Barrozzi, Milano

Galleria Forma, Genova

1975
Galleria Schema, Firenze
Galerie Vega, Liège
P.J.M. Self Gallery, London
Françoise Lambert, Milano
Oppenheim Studio, Köln
John Gibson Gallery, New York, New York, U.S.A.
Kitchen Center, New York, New York, U.S.A.
Anthology File Archives, New York, New York, U.S.A.
Galerie Yvon Lambert, Paris
Galleria Castelli, Milano
Palais des Beaux-Arts, Brussel

1976
M.L.D.'Arc Gallery, New York, New York, U.S.A.
Framartstudio, Napoli
Museum of Boymans-van-Beuningen, Rotterdam (Retrospective)
Bo Alveryd Gallery, Kavlinge, Sverige

1977
M.L. d'Arc Gallery, New York, New York, U.S.A.
CARP, Los Angeles, California, U.S.A.
H/M Gallery, Brussel
Galerie Hans Mayer, Düsseldorf
John Gibson Gallery, New York, New York, U.S.A.
Multiples Inc., New York, New York, U.S.A.
University of Rhode Island Gallery, Kingston, Rhode Island, U.S.A.
Gallery of Visual Art, University of Montana, Missoula, Montana, U.S.A.
Fine Arts Gallery, Wright State University, Dayton, Ohio, U.S.A.
Galerie Yvon Lambert, Paris

1978
Musée d'Art Contemporain, Montreal, Canada (Retrospective)
Art Gallery of Ontario, Toronto, Canada (Retrospective)
Museum of Art, University of Iowa, Iowa City, Iowa, U.S.A.
Marian Goodman Gallery, New York, New York, U.S.A.
Visual Arts Museum, School of Visual Arts, New York, New York, U.S.A.
University Gallery, College at Plattsburg, Plattsburg, New York, U.S.A.
Marianne Deson Gallery, Chicago, Illinois, U.S.A.

1979
Kunsthalle Basel, Basel
University Gallery, New York, New York, U.S.A.
John Gibson Gallery, New York, New York, U.S.A.
The Kitchen Center, New York, New York, U.S.A.
The Israel Museum, Yerushalayim
Herron Gallery, Herron School of Art, Indianapolis, Indiana, U.S.A.
Winnipeg Art Gallery, Winnipeg, Manitoba, Canada (Retrospective)
Eels Gallery, Kent State University, Kent, Ohio, U.S.A.
Musée d'Art Moderne de la Ville de Paris, Paris
Northern Illinois University, Dekalb, Illinois, U.S.A.
Françoise Lambert, Milano
Kunstverein Stuttgart, Stuttgart
Paul Roebeson Center, Rutgers University, Newark, New Jersey, U.S.A.

1980
Flow Ace Gallery, Venice, California, U.S.A.
Bruce Gallery, Edinboro State College, Edinboro, Pennsylvania, U.S.A.
Cranbrook Academy of Art, Bloomsfield Hills, Michigan, U.S.A.
Portland Center for the Visual Arts, Portland, Oregon, U.S.A.
Galerie Yvon Lambert, Paris
Pasquale Trisole, Napoli
Musée d'Art et d'Histoire, Genève

1981
Sonnabend Gallery, New York, New York, U.S.A.
Graduate center, The City University of New York, New York, New York, U.S.A.
The Contemporary Arts Center, Cincinnati, Ohio, U.S.A.
Galerie Marika Malacordia, Genève
Françoise Lambert, Milano
Lowe Art Museum, Miami, Florida, U.S.A.
Richard Hines Gallery, Seattle, Washington, U.S.A.

1982
Marianne Deson Gallery, Chicago, Illinois, U.S.A.
Rijksmuseum Kroller-Muller, Otterlo, Holland
Mills College Gallery, Oakland, California, U.S.A.
Galerie Stampa, Basel
Ikon Gallery, Birmingham
Lewis Johnstone, London

Musee d'Art et d'Histoire, Genève
Olsen Gallery, New York, New York, U.S.A.
Bonlow Gallery, New York, New York, U.S.A.
Vancouver Art Gallery, Vancouver, British Columbia, Canada
Taub Gallery, Philadelphia, Pennsylvania, U.S.A.
University Gallery of Fine Art, Ohio State University, Columbus, Ohio, U.S.A.

1983
Akira Ikeda Gallery, Tokyo
Flow Ace Gallery, Venice, California, U.S.A.
Galerie Schurr, Stuttgart
Galerie Eric Franck, Genève
Serra di Felice, New York, New York, U.S.A.
Seattle Art Museum, Seattle, Washington, U.S.A.
Munson-Williams-Proctor Institute, Utica, New York, U.S.A.
Yorkshire Sculpture Park, West Bretton, Great Britain
Whitney Museum of American Art, New York, New York, U.S.A.

1984
Braunstein Gallery, San Francisco, California, U.S.A.
Hans Mayer, Düsseldorf
Sander Gallery, New York, New York, U.S.A.
Philadelphia Art Alliance, Philadelphia, Pennsylvania, U.S.A.
Center for Contemporary Art, Palm Beach, Florida, U.S.A.
Françoise Lambert, Milano
Galerie Yvon Lambert, Paris
San Francisco Museum of Modern Art, San Francisco, California, U.S.A.
La Jolla Museum of Contemporary Art, La Jolla, California, U.S.A.
ZHTA-MI, Thessaloníki, Ellás
Visual Arts Center, Anchorage, Alaska, U.S.A.
Tel Aviv Museum, Tel Aviv

1985
Sander Gallery, New York, New York, U.S.A.
Grand Rapids Art Museum, Grand Rapids, Michigan, U.S.A.
Alan Brown Gallery, Hartsdale, New York, U.S.A.
Knight Gallery, Charlotte, North Carolina, U.S.A.
Elisabeth Franck Gallery, Knokke, Belgique

1986
Tolarno Galleries, South Yarra, Australia

Laumeier Sculpture Park St. Louis, Missouri, U.S.A.

1988
Gallery 360, Tokyo
Anne Plumb Gallery, New York, New York, U.S.A.
Walker Art Center, Seoul

1989
Paris Art Center, Paris
Galerie Yvon Lambert, Paris
Elisabeth Franck, Knokke, Belgique
John Gibson Gallery, New York, New York, U.S.A.
Willoughby Sharp, New York, New York, U.S.A.
Anne Plumb Gallery, New York, New York, U.S.A.
Holly Solomon Gallery, New York, New York, U.S.A.
Pace MacGill Gallery, New York, New York, U.S.A.

1990
Liverpool Gallery, Brussel
Pierides Museum, Athína
John Gibson Gallery, New York, New York, U.S.A.
Ace Contemporary Exhibitions, Los Angeles, California, U.S.A.
Dart Gallery, Chicago, Illinois, U.S.A.
Galerie Lohrl, Monchengladbach, Deutschland
Galerie Berndt + Krips, Köln
Galerie Joachim Becker, Cannes
Le Chanjour, Nice
Galerie Tobias Hirschmann, Frankfurt

1991
Galeria Pedro Oliveira, Porto
Landfall Press, New York, New York, U.S.A.
Galerie Friebe, Lüdenscheid, Deutschland
Galerie Gastaud, Clermont-Ferrand, France
Galerie Thierry Salvador, Paris
The Institute for Contemporary Art, Long Island City, New York, U.S.A.
Galerie Berndt + Krips, Köln
Howard Yezerski Gallery, Boston, Massachusetts, U.S.A.

1992
Blum Helman Warehouse, New York, New York, U.S.A.
University Galleries, State University of Illinois, Normal, Illinois, U.S.A.

Cleveland Center for Contemporary Art, Cleveland, Ohio, U.S.A.
Ace Contemporary Exhibitions, Los Angeles, California, U.S.A.
Galerie Marika Malacorda, Genève
Galeria Greca, Barcelona
Haines Gallery, San Francisco, California, U.S.A.
Galerie Tobias Hirschmann, Frankfurt
High Museum of Art, Atlanta, Georgia, U.S.A.
Museum of Fine Arts, Houston, Texas, U.S.A.

1993
Galerie Asbaek, København
Galerie Albrecht, München
Sala D'Exposicions, Principat d'Andorra, Andorra la Vieja
Blum Helman Gallery, New York, New York, U.S.A.
Porin Taidesmuseio, Pori, Suomi (Retrospective)
Oulu Taidesmuseo, Oulu, Suomi (Retrospective)
Ujazdoski Castle, Warszawa, Polska (Retrospective)
Weatherspoon Art Gallery, Greensboro, North Carolina, U.S.A.
Boca Raton Museum of Art, Boca Raton, Florida, U.S.A.
Galerie Renee Ziegler, Zürich
Margaret Lipworth Fine Art, Boca Raton, Florida, U.S.A.
The Fabric Workshop, Philadelphia, Pennsylvania, U.S.A.
University Art Museum, University of California at Berkeley, California, U.S.A.
Progretto, Roma

1994
Palau de la Virreina, Barcelona
Blum Helman Warehouse, New York, New York, U.S.A.
Musée D'Art Moderne de la Communauté Urbaine de Lille (Retrospective)
Joseloff Art Gallery, Hartford, Connecticut, U.S.A.
Galeria Greca, Barcelona
Galeria Aele, Madrid
Hoyt Institute of Art, New Castle, Pennsylvania, U.S.A.

1995
Galerie de la Tour, Amsterdam
Galerie Anselm Dreher, Berlin

Haines Gallery, San Francisco, California, U.S.A.
Galerie Albrecht, München
Galleria Ierimonti, Milano
Kunstsammlung Tumulka, München
Oliver Art Center, Oakland, California, U.S.A.
Butler Institute of Art, Youngstown, Ohio, U.S.A.

1996
Centre International d'Arts Visuel, Marseille
Vestsjaellands Kunstmuseum, Soro, Danmark
Galerie Asbaek, København
Archer M. Huntington Art Gallery, Austin, Texas, U.S.A.
Galerie Pro Arte, Freiburg
Galerie Lucien Durand, Paris
Mannheimer Kunstverein, Mannheim
Rijksmuseum Kroller-Muller, Otterlo, Holland
Tweed Museum of Art, Duluth, Minnesota, U.S.A.
MAMCO, Genève
Fundaçao de Serralves, Porto
Galerie Eugen Lendl, Graz, Österreich
Ota Fine Arts, Tokyo
Masataka Hayakawa Gallery, Tokyo

1997
Pilkington SIV, Porto Marghera, Venezia
Joseph Helman, New York, New York, U.S.A.
Galerie Anselm Dreher, Berlin
Stadt Galerie Nordhorn, Nordhorn, Deutschland

Group Exhibitions
1968
Dwan Gallery, "Language II-III," New York, New York, U.S.A.
Dwan Galley, "Earthworks," New York, New York, U.S.A.
Whitney Museum of American Art, "Sculpture Annual," New York, New York, U.S.A.

1969
Museum of Modern Art, "A Report-Two Ocean Projects," New York, New York, U.S.A.
Museum of Modern Art, "New Media-New Methods," New York, New York, U.S.A.
Andrew Dickson White Museum of Art, Cornell University, "Earth Art," Ithaca, New York, U.S.A.
Fernsehgalerie, "Land Art," Berlin
Stedelijk Museum, "Op Losse Schtoeven", Amsterdam

San Francisco Art Institute, "Eugenia Butler Exhibition," San Francisco, California, U.S.A.
Städtische Kunsthalle, "Prospect," Düsseldorf
Seth Siegelaub, "March," New York, New York, U.S.A.
John Gibson Gallery, "Ecological Art," New York, New York, U.S.A.
Richmond Art Center, "Return to Abstract Expressionalism," Richmond, Virginia, U.S.A.
Bern Kunsthalle, "When Attitude Becomes Form," Bern
Museum of Contemporary Art, "Art by Telephone," Chicago, Illinois, U.S.A.
Edmonton Art Gallery, "Place and Progress," Edmonton, Alberta, Canada
Jewish Museum, "The Artist's View," New York, New York, U.S.A.
Bern Kunsthalle, "Art After Plans," Bern
Seattle Art Museum, "587-087," Seattle, Washington, U.S.A.
Vancouver Art Gallery, "955,000," Vancouver, British Columbia, Canada
Galerie Swart, Amsterdam
Fort Worth Art Museum, "Contemporary American Drawings," Fort Worth, Texas, U.S.A.

1970
Chicago Art Institute, "Films-Wasash Transit," Chicago, Illinois, U.S.A.
Institute of Contemporary Art, "Against Order," Philadelphia, Pennsylvania, U.S.A.
Videogal Schum, "Identifications," Düsseldorf
Japan Art Society, "International Exhibition," Tokyo
Multiples, "Artists and Photographs," New York, New York, U.S.A.
Museum of Contemporary Art, "Evidence on the Flight of Six Fugitives," Chicago, Illinois, U.S.A.
Museum of Modern Art, "Information," New York, New York, U.S.A.
Museum of Modern Art, "Recorded Activities," New York, New York, U.S.A.
Museum of Contemporary Art, "Body," San Francisco, California, U.S.A.
New York Cultural Center, "Concept Art/Aspects," New York, New York, U.S.A.
School of Visual Arts, "Films by Dennis Oppenheim," New York, New York, U.S.A.
Parrish Museum, "Land Projects by Six Artists," South Hampton, New York, U.S.A.
Taxis Palais Gallery, "Situation/Concepts," Innsbruck, Österreich
Museo d'Arte Moderna, "Arte Povera, Concept Art, Land Art," Torino

Arts Council of Great Britain, "New Multiple Art," London
Whitney Museum of American Art, "Sculpture Annual," New York, New York, U.S.A.
Galerie Yvon Lambert, "American Drawings," Paris

1971
Boston Museum of Fine Arts, "Elements," Boston, Massachusetts, U.S.A.
Reese Palley, "Environmental Surfaces," New York, New York, U.S.A.
Françoise Lambert, Group Exhibition, Milano
Museum of Modern Art, "Pier 18," New York, New York, U.S.A.
Rijksmuseum Kroller-Muller, "Films/Sonsbeek," Otterlo, Holland
Kunsthalle Düsseldorf, "Projection '71," Düsseldorf
Biennale, Paris
Center for Art/Communication, "Art Systems," Buenos Aires
98 Greene Street, "Film, Video, Performance," New York, New York, U.S.A.
Art Museum, "Kith and Kin," University of Kentucky, Lexington, Kentucky, U.S.A.
Finch College, "Artist/Video/Performance," New York, New York, U.S.A.
Whitney Museum of American Art, "Sculpture Annual," New York, New York, U.S.A.
Stedelijk Museum, "Beyond Law and Order," Amsterdam
John Gibson Gallery, "Body," New York, New York, U.S.A.

1972
School of Visual Arts, "Performance Spaces," New York, New York, U.S.A.
Memorial Art Gallery, "Art Without Limits," Rochester, New York, U.S.A.
New York Cultural Center, "Making Megalopies Matter," New York, New York, U.S.A.
New York Cultural Center, "American Prints," New York, New York, U.S.A.
Sonnabend Gallery, "Thirteen Artists Chosen for Documents," New York, New York , U.S.A.
Incontri Internazionali d'Arte, "Persona 2," Roma
Spoleto Festival, "420 West Broadway," Spoleto (Perugia), Italia
"Encurentros en Pamplona," Pamplona, España

1973
Whitney Museum of American Art, "American

Drawings," New York, New York, U.S.A.
Sonnabend Gallery, "Drawings," New York, New York, U.S.A.
Galerie Yvon Lambert, "Actualité d'Un Bilan," Paris

1974
112 Greene Street, New York, New York, U.S.A.
Massachusetts Institute of Technology, "Interventions in Landscape," Boston, Massachusetts, U.S.A.
Bruce Gallery, "Instructions," Edinboro State University, Edinboro, Pennsylvania, U.S.A.
Kunsthalle Köln, "Project '74," Köln
Institute for Art and Urban Resources, The Clocktower, "Words and Works," New York, New York, U.S.A.
Stefanotty Gallery, "Live!," New York, New York, U.S.A.
Artist's Space, "Video Tapes," New York, New York, U.S.A.
Kennedy Center for the Performing Arts, "Art Now," Washington, D.C., U.S.A.

1975
Museum of Contemporary Art, "Body Art," Chicago, Illinois, U.S.A.
Lunds Konsthall, "Camera Art," Lund, Sverige
Passaic County Community College, "Camera Art," Paterson, New Jersey, U.S.A.
Gallery Stadler, "Body Art," Paris
New York Cultural Center, "Nude in American Art," New York, New York, U.S.A.
Museum of Contemporary Art, "Menace," Chicago, Illinois, U.S.A.
Fine Arts Building, "Self-Portraits," New York, New York, U.S.A.
Philadelphia College of Art, "Labyrinth," Philadelphia, Pennsylvania, U.S.A.
Artpark, Lewiston, New York, U.S.A.
XIII São Paolo Biennale, "Video Art," São Paulo, Brasil
Institute for Art and Urban Resources, The Clocktower, "Selections from Vogel Collection," New York, New York, U.S.A.
Institute of Contemporary Art, "Video Art," Philadelphia, Pennsylvania, U.S.A.
Kunsthalle Leben, "Art as Living Ritual," Wein
Whitney Museum of American Art, Resource Center, "Art in Landscape," New York, New York, U.S.A.

1976
Biennale di Venezia, Venezia

John Gibson Gallery, New York, New York, U.S.A.
Athens Museum, "New Art for Jimmy Carter," Athens, Georgia, U.S.A.
Institute for Art and Urban Resources, P.S.1, "Rooms," Long Island City, New York, U.S.A.
Institute of Contemporary Art, "Vogel Collection," Philadelphia, Pennsylvania, U.S.A.
Galerie Isy Brachot, "Body Art," Brussel
Louisiana Museum of Modern Art, Humlebaek, Danmark

1977
Brown University/Rhode Island School of Design, "Space Window," Providence, Rhode Island, U.S.A.
Sterling and Francine Clark Institute, "The Dada and Surrealist Heritage," Williamstown, Massachusetts, U.S.A.
Eugenia Cucalon Gallery, New York, New York, U.S.A.
Institute of Contemporary Art, "Wit and Wisdom," Boston, Massachusetts, U.S.A.
Eugenia Cuclon Gallery, New York, New York, U.S.A.
Galerie Magers Bonn, "Kunst und Architektur," Bonn
Documenta 6, Kassel, Deutschland
Palais des Beaux-Arts, "American Works from Belgium Collectors," Brussel
Philadelphia College of Art, "Time," Philadelphia, Pennsylvania, U.S.A.
The New Museum, "Early Works by Five Contemporary Artists," New York, New York, U.S.A.
Teheran Museum of Contemporary Art, Teheran
Whitney Museum of American Art, "Biennial '77," New York, New York, U.S.A
Whitney Museum of American Art, "Words," New York, New York, U.S.A.
Contemporary Arts Museum, "A View of a Decade," Chicago, Illinois, U.S.A.

1978
Centre d'Arts Plastiques, "Sculpture/Nature," Bordeaux, France
Contemporary Arts Museum, "Narrative Art," Houston, Texas, U.S.A.
Independent Curator's Incorporated, "The Sense of the Self," Washington, D.C., U.S.A.

1979
Hampshire College, "Images of Self," Amherst, Massachusetts, U.S.A.

King County Arts Commission, "Land Reclamation as Sculpture," Seattle, Washington, U.S.A.
Customs House, sponsored by Creative Time, "Custom and Culture," New York, New York, U.S.A.
Biennale, "Expansion," Wien
Institute for Art and Urban Resources, "The Great Big Drawing Show," Long Island City, New York, U.S.A.
Institute for Art and Urban Resources, "Sound," Long Island City, New York, U.S.A.
Surrey Art Gallery, "Creative Flight," Surrey, British Columbia, Canada
Musée d'National d'Art Moderne, Centre Georges Pompidou, "Video Art Symposium," Paris
Detroit Institute of Arts, "Object and Image in Contemporary Sculpture," Detroit, Michigan, U.S.A.
Art Association of Newport, "Narrative Realism," Newport, Rhode Island, U.S.A.
Aspen Center of Contemporary Art, "Portraits/Self-Portraits," Aspen, Colorado, U.S.A.
Museum of Contemporary Art, "Concept, Narrative, Document," Chicago, Illinois, U.S.A.
American Foundation for the Arts, "Storytelling in Art," Miami, Florida, U.S.A.
Marian Goodman Gallery, "With a Smile," New York, New York, U.S.A.
Akron Art Center, "Dialogue," Akron, Ohio, U.S.A.
Philadelphia College of Art, "Afterimages/Projects of the 70's," Philadelphia, Pennsylvania, U.S.A.
Akademie der Kunste, "Für Augen und Ohren," Berlin

1980
Institute for Art and Urban Resources, "Image and Object in Contemporary Sculpture," Long Island City, New York, U.S.A.
Museum of Modern Art, "Printed Art: A View of Two Decades," New York, New York, U.S.A.
Sonnabend Gallery, "Morris, Acconci, Oppenheim," New York, New York, U.S.A.
Internationale Skulpturen, Wenkenpark, Basel
ROSC International, Dublin
Wave Hill, "Temporal Structures," Riverdale, New York, U.S.A.
Los Angeles Institute of Contemporary Art, "Architectural Sculpture," Los Angeles, California, U.S.A.
University of California at Irvine, "Architectural

Sculpture," Irvine, California, U.S.A.
Center for Photography, "Reasoned Spaces," Tucson, Arizona , U.S.A.
Biennale di Venezia, "The Pluralist Decade," Venezia
Musée d'Art Moderne de le Ville de Paris, "Écouter pas les Yeux," Paris
Marian Goodman Gallery, "Dennis Oppenheim and Les Levine," New York, New York, U.S.A.
John Michael Kohler Arts Center, "cARTography," Sheboyan, Wisconsin, U.S.A.
Institute of Contemporary Art, "The Pluralist Decade," Philadelphia, Pennsylvania, U.S.A.

1981
Institute of Contemporary Art, University of Pennsylvania, "Machineworks," Philadelphia, Pennsylvania, U.S.A.
Städtisches Kunstmuseum Bonn, "Highlights," Köln
Independent Curators Inc., "Mapped Arts: Charts, Routes, Regions," New York, New York, U.S.A.
Wurttembergischer Kunstverein Stuttgart, "Natur-Skulpter," Stuttgart
Kunsthaus Zürich, "Mythos and Ritual," Zürich
Elise Meyer Gallery, "Schemes," New York, New York, U.S.A.
Rosa Esman Gallery, "Architecture by Artists," New York, New York, U.S.A.
Whitney Museum of American Art, "Biennial '81," New York, New York, U.S.A.
The New Museum, "Alternatives in Retrospect," New York, New York, U.S.A.
Espace Lyonnais d'Art Contemporain, "Les Oeuvres Plastique des Artistes de la Performance," Lyon, France
Hirshhorn Museum and Sculpture Garden, "Metaphor," Washington D.C., U.S.A.
Pratt Graphics Center, "Artists and Printmaker: Printmaking as a Collaborative Process," New York, New York, U.S.A.
Jacksonville Art Museum, " Currents: A New Mannerism," Jacksonville, Florida, U.S.A.
Neuberger Museum, "Soundings," Purchase, New York, U.S.A.
Bronx Museum, "Video Classics," Bronx, New York, U.S.A.
Aldrich Museum of Contemporary Art, "New Dimensions in Drawing," Richfield, Connecticut,
Cranbrook Academy of Art, "Instructional Drawings," Bloomfield Hills, Michigan, U.S.A.

1982
Wurttembergischer Kunstverein Stuttgart,

"Past, Present-Future," Stuttgart
Musée d'Art Moderne de la Ville de Paris, ARC 2, "Alea," Paris
Guild Hall, "Artist and Printmaker: Printmaking as a Collaborative Process," East Hampton, New York, U.S.A.
Fattoria di Celle, Pistoia
"Documenta Urbana," Kassel, Deutschland
Chicago Sculpture Society, "Mile of Sculpture," Chicago, Illinois, U.S.A.
Oakland Museum, "100 Years of California Landscape," Oakland, California, U.S.A.
Franklin Furnace, "Illegal America," New York, New York, U.S.A.
University of Southern Florida, "Currents: A New Mannerism," Tampa, Florida, U.S.A.
Creative Time Inc., "Art on the Beach," New York, New York, U.S.A.
Galerie Isy Brachot, "Art Sans Frontières," Brussel
Express/ Network, "Model Citizens Against Post-Modernism," New York, New York, U.S.A.
14 Sculptors Gallery, "Drawings, Models, Sculptures," New York, New York, U.S.A.
Gowanus Memorial Artyard, "The Monument Redefined," Brooklyn, New York, U.S.A.
Galleria Mario Pieroni, "Accardia, Oppenheim, Pistoletto," Roma
"Avanguardia Transavanguardia," Mura Aureliane, Roma

1983
Ceolfrith Gallery, Sunderland Arts Centre, "Drawings in Air," Sunderland, Great Britain
The Banff Centre, School of Fine Arts, Banff, Alberta, Canada
Tel-Hai College Art Institute, "Tel-Hai '83," Upper Galilee, Yisra'el
Palais des Beaux-Arts, "Video Art: Retrospectives/Perspectives," Brussel
Manhattan Art, "Christmas Present," New York, New York, U.S.A.
Museum of Contemporary Art, "Earthart from the Permanent Collection," Chicago, Illinois, U.S.A.
Washington Project for the Arts, "Sound Senn," Washington, D.C., U.S.A.
Kunsthaus Zürich, "Selections form the Collection," Zürich
Nationalgalerie Berlin, "Kunst mit Photographie," Berlin
Städtische Kunstmuseum Bonn, "Video," Bonn

1984
Jacksonville Art Museum, "Currents: A New

Mannerism," Jacksonville, Florida, U.S.A.
Bette Stoler Gallery, "Art Ex Machina," New York, New York, U.S.A. University Art Museum, "Bruce Nauman/Dennis Oppenheim: Drawings and Models for Albuquerque Commissions," University of New Mexico, Albuquerque, New Mexico, U.S.A.
Edith C. Blum Art Institute, "Land Marks," Bard College, Annandale-on-Hudson, New York, U.S.A
Malmö Konstall, "New Media II," Malmö, Sverige
Chicago International Sculpture Exposition, "Mile 3," Chicago, Illinois, U.S.A.
Artpark, Lewiston, New York, U.S.A.
Museum of Contemporary Art, "Selections form the Permanent Collection," Chicago, Illinois, U.S.A.
Galerie Littmann, "Dennis Oppenheim, Christo, Heinz Tesar," Basel
Québec 1534-1984, Québec, Canada
Patty Aande Gallery, San Diego, California, U.S.A.
Lehigh University Art Galleries, "Sculptural Ideas," Bethlehem, Pennsylvania, U.S.A.
Philadelphia Art Alliance, "Sculptural Ideas," Philadelphia, Pennsylvania, U.S.A.
Pennsylvania Academy of Fine Arts, "Recent Acquisitions," Philadelphia, Pennsylvania, U.S.A.
Hirshhorn Museum and Sculpture Garden, "Content: A Contemporary Focus, 1974-1984," Washington, D.C. U.S.A.
Ted Greenwald Gallery Inc., "Artist's Weapons," New York, New York, U.S.A.
Stellweg Seguy Gallery, "Soul Catchers," New York, New York, U.S.A.

1985
Whitney Museum of American Art at Philip Morris, "Modern Machines," New York, New York, U.S.A.
Palais voor Schone Kunsten, "Time: The Fourth Dimension in Art," Brussel
Symposium National de Sculpture Monumental Metallique, Thiers, France
Anne Plumb Gallery, Group Exhibition, New York, New York, U.S.A.
Hillwood Art Gallery, "The Doll Show: Dolls and Figurines," Greenvale, New York, U.S.A.
Edith C. Blum Art Institute, "The Maximal Implication of the Minimal Line," Annandale-on-Hudson, New York, U.S.A.
City Gallery, Department of Cultural Affairs, "1986: A Celebration," New York, New York, U.S.A.

1986

Elisabeth Franck Gallery, Knokke-le-Zoute, Belgique
1986: A Celebration of the Arts Apprenticeship Program, Department of Cultural Affairs, New York, New York, U.S.A.
Television's Impact on Contemporary Art, Queens Museum, New York, U.S.A.
Butler Institute of American Art, "Fireworks," Youngstown, Ohio, U.S.A.

1987

Helander Gallery, "Works of Wood," Palm Beach, Florida, U.S.A.
Charles Cowles Gallery, "Stanford Artists in New York," New York, New York, U.S.A.
Aspen Museum of Art, "Pop Art, Minimal Art, Etc.," Aspen, Colorado, U.S.A.
Corcoran Gallery of Art, "American Masters: Works on Paper," Washington, D.C., U.S.A.
Elisabeth Galasso Gallery, "Madness in America," Ossining, New York, U.S.A.
John and Mabel Ringling Museum of Art, "This is not a Photograph," Sarasota, Florida; Akron Art Museum, Akron, Ohio, U.S.A.
Laguana Gloria Art Museum, "Art That Moves," Laguana, Texas, U.S.A.
Christopher Felver, Roma
Furniture of the Twentieth Century, "Personal Visions," New York, New York, U.S.A.
Herter Art Gallery, "Contemporary American Collage 1960-1986," University of Massachusetts, Amherst, Massachusetts, U.S.A.

1989

John Gibson Gallery, "Intuition," New York, New York , U.S.A.
Mai 36 Galerie, "Art in Safe," Ruine, Genève
North Carolina Museum of Art, "Immaterial Objects," Raleigh, North Carolina, U.S.A.
The Aldrich Museum of Contemporary Art, "Project: Installation," Aldrich, Connecticut, U.S.A.

1990

Aldrich Museum of Contemporary Art, "Project: Installation," Ridgefield, Connecticut, U.S.A.
Casinò Municipale di Venezia, "Casinò Fantasma," Venezia
Albany Museum of Art, "Immaterial Objects," Athens, Georgia, U.S.A.
La Defense, "Une Collection Pour La Grande Arche," Paris
Carlo Lamagna Gallery, "Life Before Art: Images from the Age of Aids," New York, New York, U.S.A.
Exit Art, "Illegal America," New York, New York, U.S.A.
Jan Kesner Gallery, "Pharmacy," Los Angeles, California , U.S.A.
Santa Barbara, California , U.S.A.
"Exchange of Information," The Art Advisory Service, MOMA, New York, New York, U.S.A.
"Menagerie," The Art Advisory Service, MOMA, New York, New York, U.S.A.
Galerie 1900-2000, "Art Conceptuel Formes Conceptuel," Paris
Galerie Cremniter-Laffanour, "Cinq Sculpteurs Contemporain," Paris
History Museum of Lodz, "Construction in Process: Back in Lódz', 1990," Lódz, Polska
Pennsylvania Academy of Fine Arts, "Twentieth Century Realism," Philadelphia, Pennsylvania, U.S.A.
Usine de Meru,"Les Quatre Elements," Meru, France
Independent Curators Incorporated, Benefit, New York, New York, U.S.A.
John Gibson Gallery, "American Express," New York, New York, U.S.A.
Security Pacific Corporation Gallery, "The Magic Circle," Los Angeles, California, U.S.A.
Katonah Museum of Art, "The Technological Muse," Katonah, New York, U.S.A.
"Downtown Kinetic," USX Tower, Philadelphia, Pennsylvania, U.S.A.
Vered Gallery,"La Fantastique," East Hampton, New York, U.S.A.
Musée Rath, "Collections: Tinguely a Armleder," Genève

1991

Michael Klein Inc. "Trains: Burden, Kessler, Oppenheim," New York, New York, U.S.A.
The Contemporary Arts Center, "Mechanika," Cincinnati, Ohio, U.S.A.
Simposio Internacional de Escultura al Aire Libre, Madrid
IIIme Biennale de Sculpture, Monte Carlo, Principauté de Monaco
Fay Gold Gallery, "Outside America: Going into the 90's," Atlanta, Georgia, U.S.A.
The Oakland Museum, "Persona," Oakland, California, U.S.A.
Contemporary Arts Museum, "Word as Image," Houston, Texas, U.S.A.
Gallery 360, "Long, Heizer, Oppenheim," Tokyo

Galerie 1900-2000, "After Duchamp," Paris
Framartstudio, "Singolarità, L'Orizzonte Degli Eventi," Milano
Le Conseil Regional de Picardie, Amiens, France
Winnipeg Art Gallery, "Wild Things," Manitoba, Canada
Tacoma Art Museum, "Glass: Material in the Sercie of Meaning," Tacoma, Washington, U.S.A.
John Gibson Gallery,"Sixties," New York, New York, U.S.A.
Espace 2000, "Autour de la Sculpture," Arachon, France

1992

Blum Helman, "The Figure," New York, New York, U.S.A.
Blum Helman, "Nauman, Oppenheim, Serra," New York, New York, U.S.A.
Musée d'art Moderne et Contemporain, Genève
Annina Nosei Gallery, "America Mundo 1992", New York, New York, U.S.A.
Franklin Parrasch Gallery, "The Endowed Chair," New York, New York, U.S.A.
Galerie Senda, "Inauguracion," Barcelona
Musée Abbaye Saint-Leger, "Cercles," Soisson, France
Fond Regional d'Art Contemporain de Picardie, "Dessins d'Ameriques," Picardie, France
Musée d'Art Moderne de la Communauté Urbaine de Lille, Villeneuve D'Ascq, "Yvon Lambert Collections," Lille, France
"Braom: Internal Affairs," Gorinchem, Holland
Galleria degli Uffizi, "Paolo Uccello: Battles in the Art of XXth Century," Firenze
Musei di Spoleto, "Carmina Urbana," Cortona (Arezzo), Italia

1993

Gemeentemuseum Arnhem, Sonsbeek '93, Arnhem, Holland
Brooklyn Museum, "The Second Dimension: Twentieth Century Sculptor's Drawings," Brooklyn, New York, U.S.A.
Galeria Senda, "Heads," Barcelona
Helander Gallery, "The Pet Show," New York, New York, U.S.A.
Chicago Cultural Center, "The Nature of the Machine," Chicago, Illinois, U.S.A.
Turbulence, "Art/Functional Art," New York, New York, U.S.A.
Fonds Regional d'Art Contemporain de Picardie, "Portraits ," Picardie, France
Galeria Greca, "Hommage to Miro," Barcelona

Espaces Art-Defense, "Differentes Natures," Paris
Haggerty Museum of Art, Marquette University, Milwaukee, Wisconsin, U.S.A.
Aldrich Museum of Contemporary Art, "Fall from Fashion," Ridgefield, Connecticut, U.S.A.
Haines Gallery, "Body Parts," San Francisco, California, U.S.A.
Center for the Fine Arts, "Photoplay: The Chase Manhattan Collection," Miami, Florida, U.S.A.
Arts & Projects, "Leading Edge," Salzburg, Österreich
Museum of Modern Art, "Recent Acquisitions: Prints," New York, New York, U.S.A.
Musée d'Art Moderne Saint-Etienne, "La Donation Vicky Remy," Saint-Etienne, France
Centro Espositivo della Rocca Paolina, "Presenze," Perugia, Italia
Turner/Krull Galleries, "Action/Performance and the Photograph," Los Angeles, California, U.S.A.
Savage Fine Art, "It's a Beautiful Thing," Portland, Oregon, U.S.A.
Blum Helm Gallery, "The Bestiary," New York, New York, U.S.A.

1994
Städtische Galerie Goppingen, "Zuge, Zuge," Goppingen, Deutschland
The Nathan Cummings Foundation, New York, New York, U.S.A.
California Crafts Museum, "Transparency + Metaphor," San Francisco, California, U.S.A.
École des Beaux Arts de Lorient, Lorient, France
in SITE '94, San Diego, California, U.S.A./Tijuana, Mexico
Festival Iberioamericano de Teatro Bogotá, Bogotá, Colombia
Museum Schloß Mosigkau, "East of Eden," Mosigkau-Dessau, Deutschland
Galerie de la Tour, "Personal Heroes," Amsterdam
National Gallery of Art, "From Minimalism to Conceptual Art," Washington, D.C., U.S.A.
California Center for the Arts Museum, "Wildlife," Escondido, California, U.S.A.
Hill Gallery, "Popular Culture," Birmingham, Michigan, U.S.A.
Hartman & Company, La Jolla, California, U.S.A.

1995
Humphrey Gallery, "Forces," New York, New York, U.S.A.

American Fine Arts, "Mapping," New York, New York, U.S.A.
Exit Art, "Endurance," New York, New York, U.S.A.
Museum of Contemporary Art, "Reconsidering the Object of Art, 1965-1975," Los Angeles, California, U.S.A.
Biennale d'Lyon, Lyon
Phoenix Art Museum, "It's Only Rock n Roll: Currents in Contemporary Art," Phoenix, Arizona, U.S.A.
Mitzpe Ramon, "Construction in Process," Yisra'el
Hill Gallery, "Popular Culture," Birmingham, Michigan, U.S.A.
Ludwig Museum, "Sound Sculpture," Koblenz, Deutschland
The Children's Museum, "Happening," San Diego, California, U.S.A.
Newport Harbor Art Museum, "Machine," Newport Beach, California, U.S.A.
Allen Memorial Art Museum, "Action/Performance," Oberlin, Ohio, U.S.A.
Fundaçao de Serralves, "Modernism," Porto
The Whitney Museum of American Art, "Altered and Irrational," New York, New York, U.S.A.
Lawrence Gallery, "Foundations," Rosemont, Pennsylvania, U.S.A.
Presentation House Gallery, "Death and the Family," Vancouver, B.C., Canada
Burchfield-Penney Art Center, "20 Years of Hallwalls," Buffalo, New York, U.S.A.
Vered Gallery, "Food in Art," East Hampton, New York, U.S.A.
Randolph Street Gallery, "Better Living through Chemistry," Chicago, Illinois, U.S.A.

1996
Haines Gallery, "Matters of the Heart," San Francisco, California, U.S.A.
California Center for the Arts Museum, "Narcissism: Artists Reflect Themselves," Escondido, California, U.S.A.
Musée d'art moderne et d'art contemporain, "Chimeriques Polymeres," Nice
Museum of Contemporary Art, "Selections from the Collection," La Jolla, California , U.S.A.
Espace Belleville, "Outlook on Contemporary Sculpture," Paris
MAC Galeries Contemporaines des Musées de Marseille, "The Art Embodied," Marseille
Newport Harbor Art Museum, "Machine," Newport Beach, California, U.S.A.

Milwaukee Art Museum, "Landfall Press, Twenty-Five Years of Printmaking," Milwaukee, Wisconsin, U.S.A.
Alexander Soutzos Museum, "Selection from the Whitney Museum of American Art," Athína
William Patterson College, "Sensory Overdrive," Wayne, New Jersey, U.S.A.
Kunsthallen Brandts Klaedefabrik, "Trilogy- Art, Nature, Science," Odense, Danmark
Pardo View Gallery, "Sculptor's Drawings," New York, New York, U.S.A.
Mannheimer Kunstverein, "Landvermesser", Mannheim

1997
Centre Georges Pompidou, "L'empreinte," Paris
Flint Institute of Arts, "Discrimination, Cruelty and Hope," Flint, Michigan, U.S.A.
LaSalle Gallery, "Private Visions in Public Places," Charlotte, North Carolina, U.S.A.

Selected Public Collections

Akron Art Institute, Akron, Ohio, U.S.A.
Albright-Knox Art Gallery, Buffalo, New York, U.S.A.
Art Gallery of New South Wales, Sydney, Australia
Art Gallery of Ontario, Toronto, Canada
Art Gallery of South Australia, Adelaide, Australia
Art Gallery of Winnipeg, Winnipeg, Manitoba, Canada
Art Institute of Chicago, Chicago, Illinois, U.S.A
ArtPark, Lewiston, New York, U.S.A.
Atlantic Richfield (ARCO) Center for Visual Arts, Los Angeles, California, U.S.A.
Ball State University, Muncie, Indiana, U.S.A.
Bard College, Annandale-on-Hudson, New York, U.S.A.
Beuhl Foundation, New York, New York, U.S.A.
Bonner Kunstverein, Artothek, Bonn, Deutschland
Boymans-van-Beuningen, Rotterdam, Holland
Brainerd Art Gallery, State University of New York at Potsdam, New York, U.S.A.
Brooklyn Museum of Art, Brooklyn, New York, U.S.A.
Bundesgarten, Berlin, Deutschland
Cargo Centre International d'Arts Visuels, Marseille, France
Cedarhurst Sculpture Park, Mount Vernon, Illinois, U.S.A.
Centre d'Art Plastique Contemporain, Bordeaux, France
Chiba City Museum, Chiba City, Nippon
Corcoran Gallery of Art, Washington, D.C., U.S.A.
Cranbrook Academy of Art, Bloomfield Hills, Michigan, U.S.A.
Danforth Museum of Art, Farmingham, Massachusetts U.S.A.
Denison University, Granville, Ohio, U.S.A.
Denver Art Museum, Denver, Colorado, U.S.A.
Des Moines Art Center, Des Moines, Iowa, U.S.A.
Detroit Art Institute, Detroit, Michigan, U.S.A.
Edmonton Art Gallery, Edmonton, Canada
Emanuel Hoffman-Stiftung, Basel, Suisse
Everson Museum of Art, Syracuse, New York, U.S.A.
Fattoria di Celle, Pistoia, Italia
Florida Atlantic University, Fort Lauderdale, Florida, U.S.A.
Florida International University Art Museum, Miami, Florida, U.S.A.
Fonds National d'Art Contemporain, La Defense, France

Lauderdale, Florida, U.S.A.
Fort Wayne Museum of Art, Fort Wayne, Texas, U.S.A.
F.R.A.C. Nord pas-de-Calais, Lille, France
F.R.A.C. Picardie, Amiens, France
F.R.A.C. Aquitaine, Aquitaine, France
Fundaçao der Serralves, Porto, Portugal
Grand Rapids Art Museum, Grand Rapids, Michigan, U.S.A.
Groninger Museum, Groningen, Holland
Guild Hall, East Hampton, New York, U.S.A.
Haags Gemeentemuseum, Den Haag, Holland
Hallwalls Contemporary Arts Center, Buffalo, New York, U.S.A.
Helsinki City Art Museum, Helsinki, Suomi
Herbert F. Johnson Museum of of Art, Ithaca, New York, U.S.A.
High Museum of Art, Atlanta, Georgia, U.S.A.
Hiroshima City Museum, Hiroshima City, Nippon
Houston Contemporary Arts Museum, Houston, Texas, U.S.A.
Indianapolis Museum of Art, Indianapolis, Indiana, U.S.A.
Institute for Art and Urban Resources, Long Island City, New York, U.S.A.
Israel Museum, Yerushalayim, Yisra'el
Jewish Museum of Art, New York, New York, U.S.A.
Kunsthaus Zürich, Zürich, Suisse
Lannan Foundation, Los Angeles, California, U.S.A.
L'Art Contemporain au Musée Departementl des Vosges, Épinal, France
Laumeier Sculpture Park, St. Louis, Missouri, U.S.A.
Le Musée d'Art Moderne de Saint-Etienne, Saint-Etienne, France
List Visual Arts Center, Massachusetts Institute of Technology, Cambridge, Massachusetts, U.S.A.
Montclair Museum of Art, Montclair, New Jersey, U.S.A.
Los Angeles County Museum of Art, Los Angeles, California, U.S.A.
Louisiana Museum of Modern Art, Humlebaek, Danmark
Ludwig Forum fur Internationale Kunst, Aachen, Deutschland
Ludwig Museum, Köln, Deutschland
Metropolitan Museum of Art, New York, New York, U.S.A.
Milwaukee Art Museum, Milwaukee, Wisconsin, U.S.A.

Mint Museum, Charlotte, North Carolina, U.S.A.
Mississippi Museum of Art, Jackson, Mississippi, U.S.A.
Montclair Art Museum, Montclair, New Jersey, U.S.A.
Mot, The Museum of Contemporary Art, Tokyo, Nippon
Munson-Williams-Proctor Institute, Utica, New York, U.S.A.
Musée d'Art Contemporain Entrepot, Bordeaux, France
Musée d'Art et d'Histoire, Genève, Suisse
Musée d'Art Moderne de la Ville de Paris, France
Musée d'Art Moderne et d'Art Contemporain, Nice, France
Musée de Toulon, Toulon, France
Musée Grenoble, Grenoble, France
Musée National d'Art Moderne, Centre Georges Pompidou, France
Musée Royaux des Beaux Arts, Brussel, Belgique
Museum Ludwig, Köln, Deutschland
Museum of Art, Fort Lauderdale, Florida, U.S.A.
Museum of Fine Arts, Houston, Texas, U.S.A.
Museum of Contemporary Art, Chicago, Illinois, U.S.A.
Museum of Contemporary Art, Miami, Florida, U.S.A.
Museum of Contemporary Art, Honolulu, Hawaii, U.S.A.
Museum of Contemporary Art, Los Angeles, California, U.S.A.
Museum of Modern Art, Heide Park, Melbourne, Australia
Museum of Modern Art, New York, New York, U.S.A.
Museum van Hedendaagse Kunst, Gent, Belgique
National Gallery of Art, Ottawa, Canada
National Gallery of Art, Washington, D.C., U.S.A.
National Gallery of Australia, Canberra, Australia
National Museum of Contemporary Art, Kyungkido, Korea
Neuberger Museum, Purchase, New York, U.S.A.
Newark Museum, Newark, New Jersey, U.S.A.
Newport Harbor Art Museum, Newport Beach, California, U.S.A.
Niagara University, Castellani Art Museum, Niagara, New York, U.S.A.
Norton Gallery of Art, West Palm Beach, Florida, U.S.A.
Oakland Museum, Oakland, California, U.S.A.
Oberlin College, Allen Memorial Art Museum,

Oberlin, Ohio, U.S.A.
Ohio State University, Wexner Center for the Arts, Columbus, Ohio, U.S.A.
Olympic Park, Seoul
Orlando Museum of Art, Orlando, Florida, U.S.A.
Oulu Art Museum, Oulu, Suomi
Pennsylvania Academy of Fine Arts, Philadelphia, Pennsylvania, U.S.A.
Philadelphia Art Alliance, Philadelphia, Pennsylvania, U.S.A.
Philadelphia Museum of Art, Philadelphia, Pennsylvania, U.S.A.
Phoenix Art Museum, Phoenix, Arizona, U.S.A.
Pori Taidemuseo, Pori, Suomi
PS1 Institute for Art and Urban Resources, Long Island City, New York, U.S.A.
Queensland Art Gallery, Brisbane, Australia
Reina Sofia, Madrid, España
Rijksmuseum Kroller-Muller, Otterlo, Holland
Rose Art Museum, Brandeis University, Massachusetts, U.S.A.
Samsung Foundation of Art and Culture, Korea
San Diego Museum of Contemporary Art, La Jolla, California, U.S.A.
San Francisco Museum of Modern Art, San Francisco, California, U.S.A.
San Jose Museum of Art, San Jose, California, U.S.A.
Seattle Art Museum, Seattle, Washington, U.S.A.
Skulpturen Museum der Stadt Marl, Marl, Deutschland
Sohio Development Company, Cincinnati, Ohio, U.S.A.
Spencer Museum of Art, Lawrence, Kansas, U.S.A.
Sprengel Museum, Hannover, Deutschland
Staatsgalerie Stuttgart, Stuttgart, Deutschland
Stadtischer Museum Abteiberg Monchengladbach, Deutschland
Stadtisches Kunstmuseum Bonn, Bonn, Deutschland
Stedelijk Museum, Amsterdam, Holland
Tate Gallery, London
Tel Aviv Museum, Yerushalayim, Yisra'el
Tel Hai, Upper Galilee, Yisra'el
Total Art Museum, Korea
University of Alaska, Anchorage, Alaska, U.S.A.
University of California Art Museum, Berkeley, California, U.S.A.
University of Illinois Art Museum, Normal, Illinois, U.S.A.
University of Massachusetts, University Gallery, Massachusetts, U.S.A.
University of Minnesota, Tweed Art Museum, Duluth, Minnesota, U.S.A.
University of Nebraska, Sheldon Memorial Art Galleries, Lincoln, Nebraska, U.S.A.
University of New Mexico Art Museum, Albuquerque, New Mexico, U.S.A.
Ville de Thiers, Thiers, France
Wadsworth Atheneum, Hartford, Connecticut, U.S.A.
Walker Hill Art Center, Korea
Whitney Museum of American Art, New York, New York, U.S.A.
Weisman Foundation, Los Angeles, California, U.S.A.
Worcester Art Museum, Worcester, Massachusetts, U.S.A.

Bibliography

Books and Catalogs
1969
Art Povera, Germano Celant, Praeger Publishers, New York, New York
Earth Art, Andrew Dickson White Museum Of Art, Cornell University, Ithaca, New York
557, 087, Lucy Lippard, Seattle Art Museum, Seattle, Washington
Live in Your Heads: When Attitudes Become Form, Kunsthalle Berne, Bern
Op Losse Schroeven, Stedelijk Museum, Amsterdam
Prospect '69, Städtische Kunsthalle Düsseldorf, Düsseldorf

1970
Land Art, Fernsehgalerie Gerry Schum, Berlin
Concept Art/Art Povera/Land Art, Germano Celant, Praeger Publishers, New York, New York
Information, Museum of Modern Art, New York, New York
Leben und Kunst, U. Kultermann, Studio Wasmuth, Tübingen, Deutschland
955,000, Vancouver Art Gallery, Vancouver, British Columbia, Canada
Recorded Activities, Moore College of Art, Philadelphia, Pennsylvania

1971
Dennis Oppenheim, Jorge Glusberg, Centro de Arte y Communicacion, Buenos Aires
The Structure of Art, J. Burnham, George Braziller, New York, New York
Earth, Air, Fire, Water, Boston Museum of Fine Arts, Boston, Massachusetts
Concept Art, K. Honnef, Phaidon Publishers, New York, New York
Art and Life, U. Kultermann, Praeger Publishers, New York, New York
Lithographs, Nova Scotia College of Art and Design, Halifax, Nova Scotia, Canada
Multiples: The First Decade, Philadelphia Museum of Art, Philadelphia, Pennsylvania
New Multiple Art, Art Council of Great Britain, London, Great Britain
Prospect '71: Projection, Art Press Verlag, Düsseldorf
Situation Concepts, Galerie im Taxi Palais, Innsbruck, Österreich
Sonsbeek '71, Sonsbeek Foundation, Arnhem, Holland

1972
Museums in Crisis, B. O'Doherty, George Braziller, New York, New York
Il Territorio Magico, A.B. Bonito, Centro di Firenze
Documenta 5, Paul Dierichs KG & Co., Deutschland
Varieties of Visual Experience, E. Feldman, Prentice-Hall Inc., Englewood Cliffs, New Jersey and Harry Abrams, Publishers, New York, New York
Kunst van de 20e eeuw, Museum Boymans-Van Beuningen, Rotterdam, Holland
Mathias Felds Exposition, Galerie Mathias Felds, Paris
Conceptual Art, Ursula Meyer, E.P. Dutton, Publishers, New York, New York
Pop Art & Cie, F. Pluchart, Éditions Martin-Malburet, Paris

1973
Actualité d'un Bilan, Galerie Yvon Lambert, Paris
Aspects de l'Art Actuel, Centro di Firenze, Firenze
Six Years: The Dematerialization of the Art Object, Lucy Lippard, Praeger Publishers, New York, New York
Man Creates Art Creates Man, Duane Preble, Canfield Press, San Francisco, California

1974
Dennis Oppenheim, Stedelijk Museum, Amsterdam
Art Now, Artrend Foundation, Washington, D.C.
Great WesternSalt Works, J. Burnham (Ed.), George Braziller Publishers, New York, New York
Images and Icons of the Sixties, N. Calas and E. Calas, E.P. Dutton Inc., New York, New York
Senza Titllo, Germano Celant, Bulzoni Editore, Roma
Art as a Living Ritual, Pool der Poolerie, Deutschland
Kunst Bleibt Kunst, Kunsthalle Köln, Köln
Indentations, Dennis Oppenheim, Gallerie Yaki Kornblit, Amsterdam
Schema Informazione 2, Galleria Schema, Firenze
Il Corno Come Linguaggio, L. Vergine, Giampaolo Prearo Editore, Roma

1975
Dennis Oppenheim, Palais des Beaux-Arts, Brussel
Topics in American Arts Since 1945, L. Alloway (Ed.), Norton Publishers, New York, New York
American Sculpture in Progress, W. Anderson, New York Graphic Society, New York, New York
Art in Landscape, Independent Curators Incorporated, Washington, D.C.
Camera Art, Lunds Konsthall, Lund, Sverige
On ne Regards pas La Lune, Mais le Dioght qui Montre la Lune, W. de la Vaissiere, Les Ateliers de Realisations Graphiques, Paris
American Art of the 20th Century, Sam Hunter, Harry N. Abrams Publishers, New York, New York
Proposals 1967-1974, Dennis Oppenheim, Lebeer-Hossman, Brussel
The Tate Gallery, Tate Gallery Publications, Millbank, Great Britain
Video Art, Institute of Contemporary Art, Philadelphia, Pennsylvania
Video Art U.S.A., XIII São Paolo Biennale, São Paulo, Brasil
Skira Annuel, Éditions Skira S.A., Genève
The Roots and Routes of Art in the 20th Century, M. Cone, Horizon Press, New York, New York
Vito Acconci, M. Diacone, Out of London Press, New York, New York
Art in the World, S. Russell, Corte Madera, Holt, Rinehart, Winston, New York, New York

1976
Artpark: The Program in the Visual Arts, Lewiston, New York
La Biennale di Venezia (Vol. 2), Alfieri Edizioni d'Arte, Venezia
Precronistoria 1966-1969, G. Celant, Firenze
Amerikanische Kunst von 1945 bis Heute, D. Honisch and J. Jensen, Dumont Buchverlag, Köln
Modern Art and the Object, E. Johnson, Harper Row Publishers Inc., New York, New York
Open to New Ideas, Georgia Museum of Art Bulletin, Vol. 2, No. 3, Vol. 3, No. 1-3, University of Georgia, Athens, Georgia
Video Art: An Anthology, J. Schedier and B. Korot, Harcourt, Brace and Jovanich, New York, New York
Soho: Downtown Manhattan, Berliner Restwochen, Berlin
Europe/America: The Different Avant-Garde, A.B. Oliva, Deco Press, New York, New York
The Kitchen: Center for Video and Music 75-76, Haleakala Press, New York, New York

1977
American Art in Belgium, Palais des Beaux Arts, Brussel

History of Modern Art, Harry Abrams, New York, New York
Why Art, G. Battcock (Ed.), E.P. Dutton Publishers, New York, New York
The Dada and Surrealist Heritage, Sterling and Francine Clark Art Institute, Williamstown, Massachusetts
Documenta 6 (Vol. 3), Paul Dierichs KG and Company, Deutschland
Early Work by Five Contemporary Artists, The New Museum, New York, New York
Kunst und Architektur, Galerie Magers, Bonn
Art Now, Edward Lucie Smith, William Morrow and Company, Inc., New York, New York
Biennial Exhibition, Whitney Museum of American Art, New York, New York
Individuals, A. Sondheim (Ed.), E.P. Dutton Publishers, New York, New York
Video Visions, J. Price, Plume Publishers, New York, New York
Rooms P.S. 1, Institute for Art and Urban Resources, New York, New York
Space Window, Brown University, Providence, Rhode Island
Art America, M. Tighe and E. Lang, McGraw-Hill, New York, New York
Time, Philadelphia College of Art, Philadelphia, Pennsylvania
A View of a Decade, Museum of Contemporary Art, Chicago, Illinois
Skira Annuel, Éditions Skira, S.A., Genève
American Narrative/Story Art, Contemporary Arts Museum, Houston, Texas

1978
Dennis Oppenheim: Retrospective Works 1967-1977, Musée d'Art Contemporain, Montreal, Canada
Die Collectie Modern Kunst van Museum Boymans-van-Beuningen, Museum Boymans-van-Beuningen, Rotterdam, Holland
New Artists Video, G. Battcock (Ed.), E.P. Dutton, New York, New York
Artitudes, F. Pluchart, Galerie de la Marine
Artforms, D. Preble, Canfield Press, San Francisco, California
Sculptur/Nature, Centre d'Arts Plastique Contemporain de Bordeaux, Bordeaux, France
The Sense of Self, Independent Curators Incorporated, Washington, D.C.
16 Projects/4 Artists, Wright State University, Dayton, Ohio
Esthetics Contemporary, R. Kostelanetz (Ed.), Prometheus, Buffalo, New York

Topics in American Art Since 1945, L. Alloway (Ed.), Norton Publishers, New York, New York

1979
Dennis Oppenheim, Kunsthalle Basel, Basel
Dennis Oppenheim, Musée d'Art Moderne de la Ville de Paris, Paris
Dennis Oppenheim Israel Projects, Dr. Martin Weyl, The Israel Jerusalem, Yisra'el
Dennis Oppenheim Power Passage (for Indianapolis), Herron Gallery, University-Purdue University at Indianapolis, Indiana
American Art, Sam Hunter, Prentice-Hall, Englewood Cliffs, New Jersey and Harry N. Abrams Publishers, New York, New York
The Writings of Robert Smithson, N. Holt, New York University Press, New York, New York
Earthworks: Land Reclamation as Sculpture, R. G. Hess, Seattle, Washington
Image and Object in Contemporary Sculpture, Detroit Institute of Arts, Detroit, Michigan
Kollektie de Groot, Groninger Museum, Groningen, Holland

1980
Drawings The Pluralist Decade, Institute of Contemporary Art, University of Pennsylvania, Philadelphia, Pennsylvania
The Arts of Twentieth Century America, University Press of America, Lanham, Maryland
Architectural Sculpture (2 Vol.), Los Angeles, California
Printed Art: A View of Two Decades, Museum of Modern Art, New York, New York
Reasoned Spaces, Center for Creative Photography, Tucson, Arizona
Skulptur in 20, Hahrhundert, Ausstellung in Wenkenpark, Basel
Leben mit Zeitgenossen, Emanual Hoffmann-Stiftung, Basel
Für Augen und Ohren, Rene Block, Akademie der Kunste, Berlin
Wave Hill 1980: Temporal Structures, Wave Hill, Bronx, New York

1981
New Dimensions in Drawing, Aldrich Museum of Contemporary Art, Ridgefield, Connecticut
Instruction Drawings, Cranbrook Academy of Art, Bloomfield Hills, Michigan
Mythos and Ritual, Kunthaus, Zürich
Natur-Skulptur, Wurttembergischer Kunstverein, Stuttgart
Machineworks, Institute of Contemporary Art,

Philadelphia, Pennsylvania
Biennial Exhibition, Whitney Museum of American Art, New York, New York
Models and Drawings for Large Scale Sculpture, Richard Hines Gallery, Seattle, Washington
Alternatives in Retrospect, New Museum, New York, New York
The Shock of the New, R. Hughes, Knopf Publishers, New York, New York
Art in Our Times, P. Sekz, Harry Abrams Publishers, New York, New York
Schemes: A Decade of Installation Drawings, Elise Meyer Inc., New York, New York
Varieties of Visual Experience, E. Feldman, Prentice-Hall Inc., Englewood Cliffs, N.J. and Harry Abrams, New York, New York

1982
American Artists Talk on Art: From 1940-1980, E.H. Johnson, Harper and Row, New York, New York
A Concise History of World Sculpture, G. Bazin, Alpine Fine Arts Collection Ltd., New York, New York
Avanguardia/Transavanguardia, A.B. Oliva, Gruppo Editoriale Electa, Milano
'60-'80: Attitudes/Concepts/Images, Stedelijk Museum, Amsterdam
Metaphor: New Projects by Contemporary Sculptors, Hirshhorn Museum, Smithsonian Institution Press, Washington D.C.
Mile of Sculpture, Chicago Sculpture Society, Chicago, Illinois
Louisiana: The Museum and the Buildings, Louisiana Museum of Modern Art, Humlebaek, Danmark
Illegal America, Exit Art Press, New York, New York
Sichtbar Machen, Documenta Urbana, Kassel, Deutschland
Vergangenheit, Gegenwart, Zukunft, Wurttembergischer Kunstverein Stuttgart
112 Workshop/112 Greene Street, New York, New York

1983
Dennis Oppenheim, Akira Ikeda Gallery, Tokyo
Currents: Contemporary Directions in the Visual Arts, H.J. Smagula, Prentice-Hall Inc., Englewood Cliffs, New Jersey
Overlay, L.R. Lippard, Pantheon Books, New York, New York

World Art Trends 1982, J.L. Pradel (Ed.), Harry N. Abrams Inc., New York, New York
Contemporary Paintings Drawings and Sculpture, Sotheby, Parke Bernet Inc., New York, New York
Minimal, Earth and Conceptual Art, Jazzpetie, Praga
American Drawings, Watercolors, Pastels and Collages, The Concoran Gallery of Art, Washington, D.C.

1984
Dennis Oppenheim, The Tel Aviv Museum, Tel Aviv
Dennis Oppenheim, AMAM, Geneva and Erik Franck Gallery, Genève
Collection, Erika and Rouf Hoffmann, Monchengladbach, Deutschland
Chicago Sculpture International, Chicago, Illinois
Contemporary Artists, St. Martin's Press, New York, New York
Écritures dans la Peinture, Vol. 1, Vol. 2, Centre National des Arts Plastiques, Villa Arson, Nice
Land Marks, Edith C. Blum Art Institute, Bard College, Annandale-on-Hudson, New York
New Media, Malmö Konsthall, Sverige
Resource/Reservoir, San Francisco Museum of Modern Art, San Francisco, California
Sculptural Ideas, Lehigh University Art Galleries, Bethlehem, Pennsylvania
SOLS, Foundation Nationale des Arts Graphiques et Plastiques, Paris
The Art Dealers, L. deCpooet and A. Jones, Clarkson, N. Potter Inc., New York, New York

1985
Dennis Oppenheim: Accelerator for Evil Thoughts, Alain G. Joyaux, Ball State University Art Gallery, Ball State, Indiana
Sculptures, Foundation Cartier, Jouy-en-Josas, France
Symposium National de Sculpture Monumentale Metallique, La Ville de Thiers, Thiers, France
The Maximal Implications of the Minimal Line, L. Weintraub, Edith C. Blum Art Institute, Bard College, Annandale-on-Hudson, New York

1986
The Tate Gallery 1982-84, Tate Gallery Publications, Millbank, Great Britain

1987
Photography and Art, A. Grundberg and K. Gauss, Abbeville Press, New York, New York
Contemporary American Collage 1960-1986, Herter Art Gallery, University of Massachusetts, Amherst, Massachusetts

1988
Dennis Oppenheim, Walker Hill Art Center, Seoul
Beyond Modernism, Kim Levin, Harper & Row Publishers, New York, New York
Lost and Found in California. Four Decades of Assemblage Art, James Concoran Gallery, Santa Monica, California
The Turning Point: Art and Politics in 1968, Nina C. Sundell, The Cleveland Center for Contemporary Art, Cleveland, Ohio
Kroller-Muller: The First Hundred Years, Kroller Muller Museum, Otterlo, Holland

1989
Dennis Oppenheim, Elisabeth Franck Gallery, Knokke-le-Zoute, Belgique
Art in Safe, Ian Anull, Verlag Vexer, St. Gallery, Suisse
Intuition, R. Nickas, John Gibson Gallery, New York, New York
Project: Installation, The Aldrich Museum of Contemporary Art, Ridgefield, Connecticut
Art Symposium, Minos Beach, Kríti, Ellás
Photo-Kunst, Jean-François Chevrier, Edition Cantz, Stuttgart
Immaterial Objects, Richard Marshall, The Whitney Museum of American Art, New York, New York
Collection du Finds Regional d'Art Contemporain Nord PS-de-Calais, l'Associazione Culturale Italo-Francese di Bari, Mordacq, Aire-sur-la-Lys, France
Video-Skulptur Retrospektic und Aktuekk 1963-1989, W. Herzongenrath and E. Decker, Kolniescher Kunstverein, Dumont, Köln
Coming to Terms with Medieval Cypriot Ceramics through Contemporary Art, Sania Papa, The Pierdes Foundation, Larnaka, Kypros

1990
Dennis Oppenheim, Liverpool Gallery, Brussel
Dennis Oppenheim Retrospective 1970-1990, Pierides Museum of Contemporary Art, Athína
Dennis Oppenheim, Galerie Lohrl, Monchengladbach, Deutschland
Ladon: Monsters of Mythology, Bernard Evslin, Chelsea House Publishers, New York, New York
Word as Image, Milwaukee Art Museim, Milwaukee, Wisconsin

The Technological Muse S. Fillin-yeh, Katonah Musem of Art, Katonah, New York
Casino Fantasma, The Institute for Contemporary Art, New York, New York
Trains, Michael Klein Inc., New York, New York
Mondo Materials, G. Beylerian and J. Osbourne, Harry N. Abrams Inc., New York, New York
The Faces of An Era, Carlo Prosperi, Édition Sine Invest, Paris
Art Conceptual Formes Conceptuelles, M. Fleiss and C. Schlatter, Galerie 1900-2000, Paris
Une Collection pur la Grande Arche, l'Arche de la Fraternité, Paris

1991
Dennis Oppenheim: Selected Works 1967-90, Thomas McEvilley and Alanna Heiss, Harry N. Abrams Inc., and the Institute for Contemporary Art, New York
Dennis Oppenheim: Between Drinks, Galerie Gastaud, Clermont-Ferrand, France
Trains: Burden, Kessler, Oppenheim, Michael Klein Inc., New York, New York
Mechanika, The Contemporary Arts Center, Cincinnati, Ohio
Persona, The Oakland Museum, Oakland, California
Words As Image, Contemporary Arts Museum, Houston, Texas
After Duchamp, Galerie 1900-2000, Paris
There is a Minute of a Fleeting World, Fundaçao de Serralves, Porto

1992
Dennis Oppenheim: Drawings, Barbara Rose, La Difference, Paris
Dennis Oppenheim: Drawings and Selected Sculpture, Kim Levin and Peter Spooner, University Galleries, Illinois State Un., Normal, Illinois
De-Persona, Paul Tomidy, The Oakland Museum, Oakland, California
Carmina Urbana, Editrice Grafica L'Etruria, Cortona (Arezzo), Italia
Art in the Age of Aquarius, 1955-1970, William C. Seitz and Marla Price (Ed.), Smithsonian Institution Press, Washington
Collections, The Macedonian Centre for Contemporary Art, Thessaloníki, Ellás
De Bonnard a Baselitz, Estampes et Livres d'Artistes, Bibliothèque, Paris

1993
Dennis Oppenheim: Recent Works, Ministre d'Educacio, Cultura del Govern d'Andorra,

Andorra la Vieja
Art and Application, A.C. Danto, Turbulence, New York
Dolls in Contemporary Art: A Metaphor of Person Identity, Marquette University, Milwaukee, Wisconsin
La Donation Vicky Remy, Éditions du Musée d'Art Moderne, Saint-Etienne, France
The Nature of the Machine, Chicago Cultural Center, Chicago, Illinois

1994
Dennis Oppenheim, Palau de la Virreina, Barcelona
Dennis Oppenheim: Selected Works, 1967-1991, Alanna Heiss and Thomas McEvilley, Musee D'Art Moderne de la Communauté Urbaine de Lille, France *Zuge, Zuge*, Städtische Galerie Goppingen, Goppingen, Deutschland
Drawings, École des Beaux Arts de Lorient, Lorient, France
in SITE '94, San Diego/Tijuana, California/Mexico
East of Eden, Museum Schloß Mosigkau, Mosigkau-Dessau, Deutschland
From Minimal to Conceptual Art, Ruth Fine, National Gallery of Art, Washington, D.C.
Wildlife, Reesey Shaw, California Center for the Arts Museum, Escondido, California

1995
Dennis Oppenheim Obra 1967-1994, Ajuntament de Barcelona
Dennis Oppenheim: The Old In And Out, Galerie de la Tour, Amsterdam
Dennis Oppenheim, Kim Bradley, Galleria Ierimonti, Milano
It's Only Rock and Roll: Rock and Roll Currents in Contemporary Art, Prestel-Verlag, München
Reconsidering the Object of Art 1965-1975, Ann Goldstein and Anne Rorimer, The Museum of Contemporary Art, Los Angeles
Biennale de Lyon: d'art contemporain installation, cinema, video, informatique, Reunion des Musées Nationaux, France
inSITE 94, Sally Yard, Museum of Contemporary Art San Diego, Department of Culture of the City of Tijuana, California

1996
Dennis Oppenheim, Land Art 1968-78, Vestsjaellands Kunstmuseum, Storgade, Danmark
Dennis Oppenheim, Recent Sculpture and

Large Scale Project Proposals,
Art into Theatre, Nick Kaye, Harwood Academice Publishers, Great Britain
Mannheimer Kunstverein, Mannheim
Landvermesser, Mannheimer Kunstverein, Mannheim
Aus der klassischen und spaten Moderne, Alexander Duckers, Staatliche Museen zu Berlin
L'art au corps, Musées de Marseille
Chimeriques polymeres Le plastique dans l'Art du XXeme siècle, Musée D'Art Moderne et D'Art Contemporain, Nice
Artists Narcissism Reflect Themselves, California Center for the Arts Museum, Escondido, California
Regards sur la sculpture contemporaine, Espace Belleville, Confederation Française Democratique Du Travail, Paris
Art at the end of the 20th Century, National Gallery, Athína
Trilogy Art-Nature-Science, Kunsthallen Brandts Klaedefabrik, Odense, Danmark
Reel Work: Artist's Film and Video of the 1970's, Museum of Contemporary Art, Miami, Florida

1997
Dennis Oppenheim, Fundaçao De Serralves, Porto
The Private Eye In Public Art, LaSalle Partners, Charlotte, North Carolina
Blurring the Boundaries: Installation Art 1969-1996, Museum of Contemporary Art, San Diego, California
L'Empreinte, Georges Didi-huberman, Centre Georges Pompidou, Paris

Periodicals
1968
Artforum, "A Sedimentation of the Mind," R. Smithson, September, p. 44-50
Artforum, "Earthworks and the New Picturesque," S. Tillam, p. 42-45
Art News, John Gibson Gallery, Summer, p. 17
Arts, "Earth in Upheaval," P. Hutchinson, November, p. 19-21
Connaissance des Arts, "Le Rêve American: Le Grand Canyon, Les Jeunes Artistes," October, No. 200, p. 29-31
Madamoiselle, "Most Likely to Succeed," L. Lehrman, September, p. 146-149
Newsweek, "The New Art- It's Way , Way Out," H. Junker, July 29, p. 56-63
New York Post, "Art and the Artist," E. Genauer,

December 21, p. 46
New York Post, "Exhibitions not Exhibitionist," May 25, p. 37
New York Times, "An Artful Summer," G. Glueck, May 18, p. D-35
San Francisco Chronicle, "Tasteful Redition of an Old Art," T. Albright, May 29, p.23
San Francisco Examiner, J. Sanders, December 1, p. 10
San Francisco Examiner, "Art Out of Hand," S. Eichelbaum, December 1, p. 15
Village Voice, "Illusions of Reality," J. Perreault, December 26, p. 2-23
Saturday Evening Post, "Getting Down to the Nitty Gritty," H. Junker, November 2, p. 42-47
Time, "The Earth Movers," October 11, p. 84

1969
Art and Artists, "New York: Moving Out," R. Pomeroy, January, p. 56
Artforum, "Dennis Oppenheim: A Presence in the Countryside," J. Bourgeois, October, p. 34-38
Artforum, "Place and Progress," W. Sharp, November, p. 46
Artforum, "Real Time Systems," J. Burnham, September, p. 49-55
Art Gallery, "Exhibitions," February, p. 25
Art in America, "Impossible Art-What It Is," D. Shirey, May, p. 30-31
Art News, "Sweet Mysteries of Life," A. Goldin, p. 46-51
Art News, March, p. 54
Art News, "Scuba Sculpture at the Museum of Modern Art," W. Johnson, November, p. 52-53; 81
Art News: New York, "Dennis Oppenheim: Decomposition-Whitney Museum," January, p. 15
ArtsCanada, "200 Yard Dash," October, p. 38-39
Arts, "Exercises in Anti-Style," D. Ashton, April, p. 45-46
Arts, "Two Ocean Projects at the Museum of Modern Art," A. Robbin, p. 24-25
Auction, "The Expanding and Disappearing Work of Art," L. Alloway, October, p. 34-37
Casabella, "Nature Has Arisin," G. Celant, September, p. 104-107
Casabella, "Towards an A critical Criticism," G. Celant, December, p. 42-44
Combat, O. Nanteau, June 8, p. 12
Cornell Daily Sun, "Earth In ," M. Goldman, p. 20
Domus, "Prodigal Creator's Trilogy," T. Trini,

September, p. 42-55

Emmer Courant, "Kunstboer Waalkens," September, p. 80-86

Interfunktionen, "Land Art/Earth Works," F. Heubach, No. 3, p. 30

Life, "Art You Can Bank On," September, p. 80-86

L'Express, O. Hohn, June 2, p. 8

L'Oeil, "Les Grandes Vacances de L'Art Moderne," May, p. 11-19

Museumjournal, "Televisie Galerie," June, p. 138-140

New York Magazine, "The New Art-Big Ideas for Sale," R. Constable, March, p. 10

New York Times, "Painting Icebergs, Decorating Dunes," H. Kramer, November 16, p. B-25

New York Times, "Modules for the Millions," G. Glueck, June 22, p. B-32

New York Times, "Snow Projects form Canadian Borders," G. Glueck, June 22, p. 24

Nieuwsblad, V. H. Noordan, April 9, p. 10

Pariscope, "Dennis Oppenheim," B. Borgeaud, June 4, p. 10

Village Voice, "Down to Earth," J. Perreault, February 13, p. 18-20

Village Voice, "Earth Show," J. Perreault, February 27, p. 16-20

Village Voice, "Off the Wall," J. Perreault, March 13, p. 13-14

Winschoter Courant, J. H. Henssema, April, p. 7

1970

Art and Artists, November, p. 60

Art in America, "The Iceman Cometh-Symptoms of the 70's," J. Jacobs, January/February, p. 62-67

Art in America, "Something for Every Appetite," G. Glueck, March/April, p. 142-152

Art News, Summer, p. 66

Art News, "Lead Kindly Blight," D. Antin, November, p. 87-90

ArtsCanada, "Dennis Oppenheim: Catalyst 1967-1970," J. Burnham, August, p. 42-49

ArtsCanada, "World Game: The Artist as Ecologist," G. Youngblood, August, p. 42-49

Arts, "Documentizing," N. Calas, May, p. 30-32

Artweek, "Dennis Oppenheim: Conceptualist," C. McCann, November 21, p. 2

Aspen, "Art/Information/Science," No. 8, Fall, p. 12

Aspen, D. Graham (Ed.), December/January, p. 7

Avalanche, "Discussions with Oppenheim, Heizer, Smithson," W. Sharp, No. 1, Fall, p. 3

Casabella, "Archives: Dennis Oppenheim," G. Celant, No. 346, March, p. 42-44

Corriere della Sera, "Land Art and Company," February 8, p. 7

Domus, "New York," No. 487, June, p. 49-50

East Hampton Star, "Earth Art," July 30, p. 4

Flash Art, "Land Art," T. Catalano, May/June, p.17

Horizon, "The Flight from Reason," T. Meeham, Spring, p. 4-10

Interfunktionen, "Kunst Als Kontext," No., November, p. 1-41

Interfunktionen, "Dennis Oppenheim: Decompositions," No. 4, March, p. 18-29

Magazin Kunst, "Concept Art," K. Honnef, September, p. 1759-1767

National Observor, "Latest in Museums: No Walls at All," B. Marvel, August 10, p. 22

Newsweek, "Art Under Stress," D. Davis, May 2, p. 119

New York Times Magazine, "It's Called Earth Art-and Boulder-dash," R. Bongartz, February 1, p. 16-17;22-30

Robbo, "Quelques Aspects de l'Art Bourgeois," No. 5-6, p. 30

Sacramento Bee, "Conceptual Art," C. Johnson, July 19, p. 13

San Francisco Chronicle, "More Than One," T. Albright, December, p.25

San Francisco Chronicle, "Return to Earthworks," A. Frankenstein, November 5, p. 11

Studio International, "Artists and Photographs,"L. Alloway, April, p. 162-164

Time, "Back to Nature," June 29, p. 62-65

Vogue, "A Sound Enclosed Land Area," J. Gruen, August 1, p. 38

1971

Art International, E. Schwartz, December 20, p. 80

Artforum, K. Stiles, January, p. 84

Artforum, J. Tarshis, February, p. 85

Art in America, "Epilogue: The Dead Letter Office," H. Kenner, July/August, p. 104-111

Art in America, "Earthworks and Oz," D. Hickey, September, p. 40-9

Artitudes International, "Le Corps, Materiel d'Art," October, p. 1

Art News, "The Education of the Un-Artist," A. Kaprow, February, p. 28-31; 66-68

Art News, "It Reaches a Desert in Which Nothing Can Be Perceived but Feeling," D. Antin, March, p. 38-41; 66-71

Arts, L. Venturi, March, p. 48

Arts, "Subject-Object: Body Art," C. Nemser, September, p. 38-42

Art, "Media/Art/Media," D. Davis, September, p. 43-45

Avalanche, "A Discussion with Terry Fox, Vito Acconci and Dennis Oppenheim," Willoughby Sharp, Winter #2, p. 18-19

Christian Science Monitor, "And in Boston, a Child, a Parrot and Dog Join In," K. Baker, April 3, p. 4

De Groene, "Oppenheim in Galerie 20," C. Blok, November 6, p. 12

Flash Art, "Dennis Oppenheim," May, p. 12

Foto Visions, "Art Systems," August, p. 70

Haags Post, "Dennis Oppenheim Maakt Met Zijn Duim Een Hedere Piece," B. Van Garrel, October, p. 91

L'Huomoe l'Arte, "No.7," Milano, p. 5

Nuovo Indirizzo, "Dennis Oppenheim," p. 12

NRC Handelsblad, "Kunst meat Het Eigen Lichaam Als Material," L. Van Ginneken, p. 8

Opus International, "Land Art," B. Parent, March, No. 23, p. 10-27; 65-71

Rolling Stone, "Art Conceptual, Media, Processed and Forced on a Bun-No Relish," T. Albright, June 24, p. 40-41

San Francisco Chronicle, "Black Rock, Beams and Bones," A. Frankenstein, February 7, p. 11

San Francisco Art Chronicle, "The Urban Design Plan for San Francisco," A. Frankenstein, June 27, p. 15

Siete Dias, "Nadie Entiende me Obra Ni Yo Tampoco," V. Rabin, October, p. 50-51

Studio International, "Interview with Dennis Oppenheim," W. Sharp, November, p. 183-193

Village Voice, "Protection," October 21, p. 35

Woensdag, "Dennis Oppenheim: Houdt van Directe Emoties," L. Van Duinhoven, November 3, p. 6

1972

Artforum, "Talking to Pomona," D. Antin, September, p. 36-47

Art News, "Education of the Un-Artist," A. Kaprow, May, p. 34-39

Arts, "Interactions: Form-Energy-Subject," Dennis Oppenheim, p. 36-39

Arts, R. Matthias, Summer, p. 58

Arts, R. Mattias, November, p. 68

Art International, E. Schwartz, Summer, p. 128

Craft Horizons, December, p. 61

Der Spiegel, "Nach Pop Ein Babylon der Kunst," March, p. 149

Interfunktional, June, p. 63

New York Times, "Sculptuama," G. Glueck, June 11, p. B-23
On Site, "Non-focality," A. Sky, p. 7
Opus International, June, p. 63
San Francisco Chronicle, "187 Hot Hub-Thievery for Art's Sake," January, p. 17
Times Union, "Art Without Limit," L. Hansen, April 7, p. 1

1973
Art and Artists, "Dennis Oppenheim: Myth and Ritual," Lenore Goldberg, August, p. 22-27
Art in America, K. Baker, May, p. 103
Artforum, R. Smith, April, p. 85-86
Art News, February, p. 72, 81
Arts Review, October, p. 20-21
Arts, "Renewal of Possibilities," L. Goldberg, November, p. 42-43
Arts, "Open to Re-definition," J. Loring, November, p. 42-43
Chroniques de l'Art Vivant, "Dennis Oppenheim," I. Lebeer, June, p. 13-15
Flash Art, February, p. 20-21
Fuoricampo, "Passaggio Ambiente e Gesto Nella Land Art," L. Vergine, July/August, p. 20-22
El Nacional Carasas, "Dennis Oppenheim: Arte Impossible," July, p. 8
Evening Standard, R. Cork, September, p. 20
L'Art Vivant, "Le Corps de l'Oevre du Corps," I. Lebeer, June, p. 7
Magazin Kunst, "Documentation #15," M. Jochimse, January, p. 60
Studio International, "Interview with Dennis Oppenheim," Hershman, November, p. 196-197
Studio International, S. Kent, November, p. 197-198
XXe Siècle, "Cinema et Video," B. Borgeaud, December, No. 4, p. 154

1974
Art and Artists, January, p. 42
Artforum, S. Heinemann, September, p. 85
Artforum, R. Smith, May, p.71
Artitudes, "Notes Sur l'Art Corporal," F. Pluchart, No. 12/14, p. 65
Art News, "Back to Nature," E. Driscoll, Jr., September, p. 80-81
Art-Rite, "Rehearsal for Five Hour Slump," Dennis Oppenheim, Fall, No. 7, p. 20
ArtsCanada, "Borderlines in Art and Experience," J. Bodolai, Spring, p. 65-81
Avalanche, "Performance," May/June, p. 5
Cles Pour les Arts, "Bruxelles: Happening, Dennis Oppenheim," J.P. Tigem, October, p. 10

Chroniques de l'Art Vivant, "Projekt," I. Lebeer, July/September, p. 11
Dance, "The Arts in Fusion," P. Frank, April, p. 56-57
Data, "Dennis Oppenheim," L. Venturi, Fall, No. 13, p. 77-79
Feuilleton, "Die Unsichtuaren Tiefenschicheen der Energie," G. Jappe, April, p.5
Magazin Kunst, "Interview with Dennis Oppenheim," W. Sharp, January, p. 114
Magazin Kunst, "Documentation #19," G. Schwarzbauer, January, p. 64
Print Collector's Newsletter, "Words in Print," P. Larson, July/August, p. 53-56
Studio International, R. Kennedy, December, p. 252
Studio International, E. Cameron, December, p. 245-248

1975
Art and Artists, G. Battock, June, p. 22
Art and Cinema, Vol. 2, No.1, p. 2
Artforum, "Pygmalion Reversed," M. Kosloff, November, p. 30
Artforum, M. Kosloff, November, p. 30
Arts in Society, "De-Architectuization," J. Wines, Fall/Winter, p. 351-363
Arts International, September, p. 58
Arts in Ireland, "Dennis Oppenheim," June, p. 46-48
Artitudes International, "L'Art Corporal," F. Pluchart, January-March, No. 18-20, p. 10
Arts, "Dennis Oppenheim: An Art with Nothing to Lose," K. Baker, April, p. 72-74
Arts, March, p. 19-20
Domus, "Art in America," G. Battock, May, p. 534
Goya, November, No. 129, p. 178-179
Skanska Dagbladet, January, p.24
Skira Annuel, "Dans le Courant de l'Art Conceptual," p. 38-39
Soho Weekly News, "Soul Food for Thought at the Kitchen Table," M. da Vinci, October 2, p. 11
Soho Weekly News, M. da Vinci, January 9, p. 7
Studio International, "Space as Praxis," R. Goldberg, September, p. 132
Studio International, B. Baker, September, p. 164
Village Voice, "Far Out and Far In, Uptown and Down," D. Bourdon, January 20, p. 94

1976
Artforum, A. Kingsley, February, p. 72-73
Artforum, N. Foote, April, p. 54-57

Artforum, "Drawing the Line," N. Foote, May, p. 54-57
Artforum, "The Anti-Photographers," N. Foote, September, p. 46-54
Artforum, "The Size of Non-Size," D. Davis, December, p. 46-51
Art in America, P. Derfner, May-June, p. 105-106
Arts, L. Lorber, April, p. 19
Art International, "The Modern Maze," D. Onorato, April/May, p. 21-25
Art International, "Modern Maze Makers," J. Kardon, April, p. 66
Art International, "The 37th Venice Biennale," H. Martin, September/October, p. 14-24, 59
Art News, E. Perlmutter, April, p. 67
Domus, July, No. 560, p. 53
Domus, "I Topi di Oppenheim," March, No. 556, p. 53
Domus, "La Biennale di Venezia," R. Barilli and G. Battcock, November, No. 564, p. 1-20
Du, "Sport in der Zeitgenossischen Kunst," B. Braathen, p. 62-63
Flash Art, May-June, No. 64-65, p. 3, 21-28, 42-46
Museum Journal, "Kunstkritiek en de Veelzijde lijfelijkheid van Body Art," T. Zandee, February, p. 97-106
New York Times, J. Russell, February 15, p. B-35
New York Times, J. Russell, October 1, p. B-30
New York Times, "Far-our Art to Honor Carter Donated to a Museum," G. Glueck, December 6, p.66
Studio International, "Annihilating Reality," G.P. Orridge and P. Christopherson, July/August, p. 44-48
Studio International, "Music of Signs in Space," November/December, p. 284-285
Soho Weekly News, M. da Vinci, January, p. 29

1977
Artforum, "Madness in the Arena," N. Calas, September, p. 51-53
Artforum, "I Shot the Sheriff," R.J. Onorato, November, p. 71-72
Art in America, "The American Artist from Loner to Lobbyist," C. Ratcliff, March-April, p. 10-12
Arts, V. Tatransky, September, p. 21
Arts, B. Cavaliere, May, p. 24
Arts, A. Ellenzweig, June, p. 33
Art News, E. Schwartz, September, p. 99
Atlanta Journal, "Artists Saluting Carter to

Discuss Work," W. Burnett, January, p. 2
Craft Horizons, August, p. 65
Cue, L. Harnett, November 25, p. 40
Domus, August, No. 573, p. 54
New York Magazine, "Ceremonies of Measurement," T.B. Hess, March 21, p. 60
New York Times, "Far Out Art to Honor Jimmy Carter," G. Glueck, December 16, p. 11
New York Times, "The New Museum Where Small is Beautiful," J. Russell, November 11, p. C-17
Parachute, "It Ain't What You Make, It's What Makes You Do It," Winter, p. 10-12
Studio International, "Art Outdoors-In and Out of the Public Domain," L. Lippard, p. 83-90

1978
Artforum, "Bodyworks and Porpoises," N. Calas, January, p. 33
Artforum, Edit de Ak, Summer, p. 76
Artforum, "Dennis Oppenheim's Delirious Operations," J. Crary, November, p. 36-40
Art International, "Teheran, The New Museum," E.H. Johnson, April/May, p. 11-17
Art News, K. Larson, December, p. 144
Arts, "Dennis Oppenheim: Post-Performance Works," K. Levin, September, p. 122-125
Boston Phoenix, "Making Light of Heavy Art," K. Baker, January 16, p. 11
Domus, March, No. 580, p. 48
Domus, October, No. 587, p. 45-46
Globe and Mail, "Art of Enquiry," P. White, September 16, p. 33
Macleans, "Modern Mystic, Witty Prophet," M. Weiler, October 23, p. 50
New York Arts Journal, "Dennis Oppenheim: An Interview," S. Morgan, November/December, p. 29-30
The Review, "Returning Relevance," R. Rhodes, September 21, p. 6
Toronto Star, "Concrete Poet of the Contemporary World," G.M. Dault, September 21, p. 4
Vie des Arts, Summer, p. 6
Village Voice, "Dennis Oppenheim's Dilemma," R. Goldstein, January, p. 16

1979
American Artist, "Artist in Residence: Dennis Oppenheim," R. Fitzgibbons, January, p. 60-63;93-95
Artforum, H. Foster, May, p. 64
Artforum, "Monument-Sculpture-Earthwork," N. Foote, October, p. 32
Artforum, "Nothing/ Not Nothing/ Something,"

J. Masheck, November, p. 42-49
Artscribe, "Gut Reaction," S. Morgan, Spring, p. 34
Arts Exchange, "Interview with Dennis Oppenheim," M. Bopp, January/February, p. 13
Arts, V. Tatransky, May, p. 36
Atlanta Art Papers, "Interview with Dennis Oppenheim," D. Talley, September/October, p. 1-4
Basler Zeitung, "Dennis Oppenheim Inder Basler Kunsthalle," B. Cuiger, June 2, p. 13
Connaissance des Arts, "Ex-centrivites," December, No. 334, p.55
Das Kunstwerk, J. Halder, October, p. 81-82
Der Spiegel, "Wuste in Lieb," June 11, p. 183
Du, June, No. 6, p. 27
Flash Art, "Dennis Oppenheim," P. Fend, January/February, p. 42
Flash Art, "Die Tottenstadt Eine Architektur Nach Dennis Oppenheim," P. Fend, June/July, p. 10
Flash Art, October/November, p. 52
Feilleton, "Psycho-Installationen a la Duchamp and Hitchcock," H. Reuther, September, p. 10
Impulse, "I Shot the Sheriff," Dennis Oppenheim, Spring, p. 12
Journal de Genève, "Exposition a Bale," P. Mathonnet, June, p. 15
Kunsat Magazin, "Neue Installationen 1978-1979," J.C. Ammann, June, p. 24-33
Kunstforum International, A. Pohlen, No. 4, p. 240
L'Agina, "A New Aesthetic," B. Oldenburg, March 1, p. 17
Landscape Architecture, "Earthworks in Seattle: Reclamation as a Fine Art," G. Clay, May, p. 291
New Jersey Architecture, "Interview," D. Wall, July/August/September, p.1
New York Times, "Custom-Made," J. Perreault, May 4, p. 46
New York Times, "Artists of the Customs House," G. Glueck, May, p. C-21
New York Times, G. Glueck, March 16, p. C-24
New York Times, "Triple-Header in Newark," V. Raynor, October 14, p. B-20
Paletten, "Kontens Satellitresa och de Intuitiva Strategierna: Ett Samtal med Dennis Oppenheim," O. Hjourt, Vol. 4, p. 32-38
The Arts, "King County's Earthworks Symposium Breaking New Ground With Land Reclamation as Sculpture," G. Clay, July, p. 1-2
The Winnipeg Art Gallery Report, "Dennis Oppenheim: Works 1967-1977," July, p. 2

Vanguard, "Conjectural Imaging," W. Klepac, October, p. 12
Village Voice, "The Thought That Counts, P. Frank, March 13, p. 61

1980
Artes Visual, Carla Stellweg, May, p. 27
Artforum, I. Puliafite, February, p.107
Artforum, "A Chronology of Video Activity in the United States: 1965-1980," B. London and L. Zippay, September, p. 42-45
Art in America, "Cost-Effective Earth Art," B. Noah, January, p. 6
Artistes, J. Poi, February/March, p. 40
Art News, M. Staniszewaski, September, p. 248-249
Arts, V. Tatransky, May, p. 33-34
Arts, J. Herman, June, p. 33
Arts, "The Space of the Self: Robert Morris' In the Realm of the Caraeral," S.Eisenman, September, p.104-109
Artspeak, "New Concepts in Environmental Sculpture," A. Zito, March 27, p. 6
Artweek, "Searching for Clues," B. Fahr, D. Hochofen, February, No.2, p. 85
Artweek, "Images as Information and Experience," M. Johnstone, May, p.11-12
Artworld, M. Meyer, March/April, p.7
Domus, "Dennis Oppenheim," B. Marcelis, March, No.604, p. 56
Du, "In Jenen Ideen Geschiedet Werden," D. Hochofen, February, No.2, p. 85
Eccentric Birmingham-Bloomfield Edition, "Sculpture Destined to Make Art History," C. Abatt, April 17, p. B-1-C
Flash Art, V. Tatranslky, March, No. 96-97, p. 22
Landscape Architecture, "Earthworks Move Upstage," G. Clay, January, p. 55-57
La Quinzainelitteraire, "Les Factories de Dennis Oppenheim," G. Raillard, January 1, p.19
Tribune de Genève, "Les Exposition a Paris-Les Usines de Dennis Oppenheim, D. Cornu, January 8, p. 25
Le Figaro, "Les Grandes Energies de Dennis Oppenheim," January 11, p. 26
Le Figaro, "Liberte Frande," M. Nuridsany, January 4, p.28
Le Matin, "Dennis Oppenheim a l'Arc," M. Bouisset, January 7, p. 4
Le Monde, "Dennis Oppenheim a l'Arc," January 3, p.11
Le Nouvel-Observateur, "A l'Arc- Dennis

Oppenheim," F. Auser, January 5, p. 6
Los Angeles Herald, "A Sculptor's Mystical Machine, "C. Synder, April 29, p.C-14
New York Post, "The Week in Review-Art," J. Tallmera, January 15, p.14
New York Times, G. Glueck, January 11, p. C-17
New York Times, J. Russell, March 21, p. C-21
Opus International, "Petit Lexique en Forme de Puzzle," Spring, No. 76, p.36
Paris-Hebde, D. Boone, January 9, p.11
Soho Weekly News, "Keeping An Image," J. Perreault, January 3, p.33
Southfield Eccentric, "Sizable Sculpture, Southfield Builder Aids Project," C. Abatt, April 17, p.2
Village Voice, "Metaphysical Attraction," K. Larson, March 17, p.79

1981
Art Express, K.S. Friedman, May/June, p.77
Artforum, S. Morgan, Summer, p. 97-98
Artforum, "Labyrinths: Tradition and Contemporary Works," H. Kern, May, p. 60-68
Art In America, "American Quartet," R. Morris, December, p. 63
Art News, "Artist's Go On Record," P. Frank, December, p. 80
Arts, B. Cavaliere, May, p. 33
Arts, "Robert Smithson and Film: The Spiral Jetty Reconsidered," P. Childs, October, p. 56
Arts, "The Factories," E. Braun, June, p.138-141
Arts, "An Interview with Dennis Oppenheim," S. Wood, June, p.133-137
Artweek, "Metaphors of Esoteric Procedures," R. Glowen, October, p. 3
Benzene, "Image Processing Factories," R. Becker, Summer, p. 20
Cincinnati Inquirer, "Oppenheim Created Thinking Machines," O. Findsen, March 19, p. K-771
Cincinnati Post, "Machine Sculptures Express Workings of the Artist's Mind," B.J. Friedman, March 26, p. 3-C
Dialogue, J. Jordan, March/April, p. 8
Dialogue, "Constructions II: Dennis Oppenheim," N. Felshin, March/April, p.19-21
La Vie Protestance, L. Favre, January 9, p. 14
Miami Herald, H.L. Kohen, September 6, p. 2L
Seattle Times, S. Kendall, October 3, p. B6
Tribune de Genève, "L'Aventure Dennis Oppenheim a Genève," H. Teicher, January 18, p. 21

Village Voice, K. Levin, February 18-24, p. 74
Rampike, "Wood," Dennis Oppenheim, Spring, p. 8

1982
Artforum, T. Lawson, September, p. 78
Art Monthly, "Dennis Oppenheim," R. Ayers, May, p.17-19
Art News, "Art Between Mind and Matter," E. Schwartz, December, p. 56-61
Artscribe, S. Morgan, June, p. 60-62
Art World, "Rockets Red Glare," J. Tully, Summer, p. 7
Basler Zeitung, S. Gassert, June, p. 9
Express Newspaper, S. Falcon, Fall, p.17
Flash Art, Summer, p. 82
Guardian, "A Sculptor Who Plays with Fire," I. McManus, May, p.12
Kunstechos, "Kroller-Muller Beeldentuin," March/April, p.11
Tribune de Genève, "La Sculpture d'Oppenheim n'ira pas as Parc Bertrand," March, p. 27
La Suisse, "Alors, Oppenheim," March 27, p. 26
Life Magazine, "Sculpture with a Short Fuse," October, p.133-135
New York Magazine, "Apocalypse Now," K. Larson, June 14, p. 50-54
New Art Examiner, "The Mechanical Obsession," A.J. Metaphor, February, p.10-11
Rampike, "Violence," K.E. Jirgens (Ed.), Vol. 2, No. 3, p. 9-13
Time Out, "Mutants, Machines, Make-Believe," S. Kent, May 7, p.16
Vanguard, D. Jowlett, December/January, p. 23

1983
Anchorage Times, "Exploding House," J. Holloweel, September 25, p. 26
Art Das Kunstmagazin, Fattoria di Celle, August, p.84
Arte, "La Fabbrica dei Capolavori," Cabutti, February, p. 65
Art in America, Jonathan Crary, January, p.87
Artweek, "Mechanical Confrontations," K. Norklum, March, p.26
Bomb, "Sculpture and Fiction," April, p. 33
Calgary Herald, "Installations," N. Tousley, August 4, p. F6
Express, "Dennis Oppenheim's Infinitely Ambiguous Objects," Don Wall, August/September, p. 8
Japan Times, B. Thoren, February 27, p. 7
Juliet, "Dennis Oppenheim," April/May, p.17-19

Studio International, "Interview with Dennis Oppenheim," Dorothy Walker, vol. 196, no. 999, p. 39-41
Tableau, "Recent Works of Dennis Oppenheim," J. Robinson, Summer, p. 406-410

1984
Anchorage Times, "University Sculpture Reflects Artist's Unconventional Flair," R. Gluckman, November 18, p. E-5
Anchorage Times, "Artist Takes Offense at Fenced-in Sculpture," R. Gluckman, November 8, p. A-1
Anchorage Times, "Swirling Sculpture," October 10, p. 7
Anchorage Times, "Sculpture Provokes Diverse Response," R. Gluckman, November 3, p. B-5
Anchorage Daily News, "Metal Sculpture," D. Stabler, November 11, p. 1-6
Artforum, Donald Kuspit, May, p. 85
Artforum, Donald Kuspit, December, p. 96
Artweek, "Dennis Oppenheim and the Eternal Machine," C. Simmons, May 19, p. 1
Arts Magazine, T. Lichtenstein, April, p. 71
Buffalo Evening News, "Works That Move You," R. Morgan, September 24, p. 13
Chicago Tribune, May 11, p. 32
Democrat and Chronicle, "Works That Move You," R. Morgan, July 14, p. D-1
Flint Journal, J. Harvey, October, p. F-1
High Performance, "Trunks of the Mind," M. Miffin, Vol. 8, #4, p. 12
Jerusalem Post Magazine, "Machinations of the Mind," G. Goldfine, September 26, p.E-2
Northwest Orient, "Frontiers of Culture," April, p. 11
Potsdam State University Newsletter, L. Cania, August 22, p. 5
San Francisco Examiner, "The Brainstorming Think-Pieces of D.O.," A. Morch, May 28, p.7
San Francisco Chronicle, "Sculptor's Factories of Thought," K. Regan, May 31, p.64
Syracuse Herald, "Oppenheim's 'Machine-Works' Give Structure to Concepts," S. Chayat, July 8, p. 2
Syracuse Herald, "And Just Marvelous," R. Hammond, July 13, p.D-13
Syracuse Post Standard, "Artwork May Soon Go Over with a Bang," J. Barth, August 28, p. B-2
Syracuse Daily News, "Machine as Metaphor," T. Tilton, September, p. 9
The Tribune, "Artist's Machines Mirror human Foibles," C. Shore, June 1, p. D-1
Visual Art, "Puer Aeternus: The Eternal Boy in

Art," B. Brown, Summer, p. 45
West Art, "Experimenting with New Forms," May 25, p. 8
Watertown Daily Times, "Sculpture Explodes While 6,000 Watch," S. Billmyer, August 30, p. 1

1985

Ball State Daily News, "Artists Comments on Themes of Anarchy, Irrationality in Works," S. Uptgraft, April 4, p.6
Citizen's Journal Press, "Ground breaking Gala on Tap for OSU's Visual Arts Center," L. Edwards, September, p. 11
Grand Rapids Press, "Oppenheim to Lecture at Art Museum," August 25, p. 9
Grand Rapids Post, "Dennis Oppenheim's Piece is a Delight at Art Museum," M. Pierce, September 2, p. 7
Michigan Press, "Artist to Lecture at Art Museum," August 28, p. 287
Michigan Press, "Large Sculpture Shoen at GR Museum," August 23, p.287
Michigan Press, "Exhibition Features Inventions," July 31, p. 6
Michigan Press, "Sculptor Scheduled for Museum Lecture," September 3, p. 3
Newsletter: Grand Rapids Art Museum, Grand Rapids, Michigan, September-October, p. 2
Ohio State Lantern, "Senior Class Gift Is First of a Series," J. O'Connor, August 9, p. 3
The New York Times, Vivian Raynor, March 15, p. C-18
Village Voice, "Dennis Oppenheim: Project Drawings," G. Trebay, April 2, p. 35
Visitor, "Dream Factory," August-September, Vol. 17, p. 23

1986

Pittsburgh Post Gazette, "Need for Self-Analysis Exhibited in Ohio Show," D. Miller, October 4, p. 11
Plain Dealer Cleveland, "Metal Works Exhibit Shows Artist's Mettle," H. Cullinan, December 6, p. 21-A
St. Louis Post Dispatch Sunday Magazine, P. Degener, September 14, p. 22
St. Louis Post Dispatch, "Oppenheim Drawings Shown at Laumeier," J. Harris, May 30, p. 48
Vindicator, "Launching Structure," October 2, p. 4

1987

Austin-American Statesman, "Art That Moves," M. McCombie, March 19, p. G3
Daily Texan, "Power of Movement Pevades

Laguna Exhibit," L. Foerster, April 2, p. 10
Milwaukee Journal, "Nuts and Bolts of Art," J. Auer, August 2, p. 14E
New Art Examiner, "Eccentric Machines," J. Schultz, September, p. 55
Seattle Post Intelligencer, "Nuts and Bolts Art," R. Hackett, June 12, p. 1
The New York Times, "American's Sculpture Will Top West Berlin Gate," February 15, p. 73

1988

Anchorage Times, "Art Talk," Karen Stahlecker, October 23, p. F1
Arts, P. Cyphers, October, p.105
Artweek, "Out of Context," R. Dolnit, April 17, p. 1
East Hampton Star, "Olympic Sculpture," June 30, p.16
Korea Times, "2nd Int'l Open Air Sculpture Symposium Produces Works of Metal Composites," I. Kim, April 30, p. 28
New York Press, R. Mahoney, August 5, p. 8
The New York Times, M. Kimmelman, August 19, p. 33
The New York Times, "For the 60's Devotees, A Show Fraught with Nostalgia," J. Russell, November 27, p. 36
The New York Times, "A Potent Look Back at 1968: A Visual Memory of Social Change," William Zimmer, November 27, p. 36
Village Voice, "Sleeper's Awake?", J. Perreault, December 13, p.113

1989

Art in America, Calvin Reid, July, p.101
Art News, Eleanor Heartney, April, p.202
Artforum, David Rimanelli, April, p.101
Arts, Robert Morgan, April, p.96
Beaux-Arts, "Dennis Oppenheim," Vanessa Costa, March, p.88
Los Angeles Times, "An Artful Turnaround," H. Harper, January 16, p.18
New Art International, "The Theatre of Memory," A. Izzo, Summer, p.16
New Art International, Carlo Prosperi, Summer, p. 24
New York Times, "The Aldrich Fills It's Rooms with Expansive Sculptures," William Zimmer, November 12, p. 35
New York Times, "Kinetic Sculpture Using Toys, Fire and Water," Roberta Smith, January 20, p. C24
Splash, "Ghosts in the Machine," Tobey Crockett, February, p. 80-87

1990

Artweek, "Encounters with the Imagination," M. Timberman, April 26, p.12
Contemporeana, "Dennis Oppenheim," Sania Papa, September, p.95
Diagonals, Olivier Zahm, November-December, p.33-37
Galeries Magazine, "Dennis Oppenheim," Sania Papa, February-March, p. 82-85
L'Express, "La Mecanique d'Oppenheim," Guy Gilsoul, October 5, p.165
Los Angeles Reader, "Documentary Art from Caves to Conceptualism," L. Andreoli-Woods, May 18, p. 13
Tableau, "D.O. Slaat Niewe Weg In," Marlot Bloemhard, October, p.124-128
Village View, "Nudge, Nudge, Wink, Wink," Vol. 4, June 15, p. 29
Village Voice, Kim Levin, May 29, p.112
Westdeutsche Zeitung, Heike Bynm, March 5, p. 7

1991

Artforum, "The Dark Side of Dennis Oppenheim," Tobey Crockett, December, p. 68-73
Art Press, Paul Ardenne, October, p. 94
Dialogue, "Mechanike," Jan Riley, May-June, p. 36
Feuilleton, "Land Art: Landschaft als Kunst," February 8, p. 8
Flash Art, Luk Lambrecht, March-April, p.149
Het Parool, "Saboterende Kamikaze-piot," Ijsbrand Van Veelen, June 28, p.11
Lapis, "Art as Imperative," Bernardo Pinto de Almeida, March, p. 42-50
Ludenscheider Nachrichten, "Land Art: Landochaft als Kunst," Britta Hueck-Ehmer, February 8, p. 16
Newsday, "Mixing Stars, Stripes and Statements," Alistair Gordon, July 10, p. 4
Sculpture Magazine, "Stalking the Invisible," Tobey Crockett, March-April, p. 40-47
Rogue #8, Interview, January 2, p. 29
The New York Times, Phyllis Braff, July 7, p.12
Tema Celeste, "A Conversation with Tricia Collins & Richard Milazzo," March/April, p. 68-74
The New York Times, "Rebuking Tradition," Michael Kimmelman, December 20, p. C18
The Journal of Art, "Existential Collisions and Ghostly Herds," Calvin Reid, December, p.39-42

1992

Atelier, "Wishing the Mountains Madness," Kay

Larson, April, p. 4-21
Arts, Dorothy Spears, March, p. 74
Artnews, George Melrod, March, p. 123
Los Angeles Times, Susan Kandel, April 3, p. 16
New York Newsday, "Cold War Politics Meets the Art Scene," Amei Wallach, January 7, p. 4-81
New York Magazine, "High Wire Act," Kay Larson, January 6, p. 52-53
Parkett, "A Poesy of Diagnostics or the Object-Neurology of Dennis Oppenheim," Roger Denson, p. 20-29
The Pantagraph, "Artwork Gives Sense of Mystery and Fun," Spencer Sauter, March 20, p. C2

1993
Artspace, "Looking for Love Gas," Tobey Crockett, March/April, p. 46-49
Art Press, Eleanor Heartney, January, p. 12-19
Clockwatch Review, "The Storm at the End of the Rainbow," James Plath, Vol. 8, p. 113-123
Shift Fifteen, Maria Porges, Vol. 7, p. 52-55
SPOT, "Dennis Oppenheim: No Photography," Alison de Lima Greene, Spring, p. 3

1994
Arte, "Dennis Oppenheim: Recent Works," Francesc Miralles, December, p. 32-33
ArtNews, "When Artists go to the Movies," Paul Gardner, December, p. 124
Casting, "Dennis Oppenheim," Franco di Matteo, March, p. 42-43
Culture, "Just Add Water," Paul Aho, March-May, p. 2-4
Da Giovedì "The Black Humor of Oppenheim," Patrizia Ferri, January, p. 19
Flash Art International, Laura Cherubini, March, p. 76
Kiosk, "An Interview with Artist Dennis Oppenheim," J.W. Morson, Spring, p. 8-12
La Vanguardia, Juan Bufill, November, p. 36
La Vanguardia, Olga Spiegel, November, p. 48
Olympic, "Suite Olympic Centennial: Oppenheim," Mercedes Basso, November, p. 26
Parachute, Sherry Gache, November, p. 45
Sculpture, Valerie Mavridorakis, October/December, p. 44-45
The Hartford Courant, "Artist Sees Beauty in the Bothersome," Jocelyn McClurg, August, p. E-1.
The New York Times, William Zimmer, October 2, p. 18.

1995
Amsterdams Nieuws, "Voor harde beelden ben id de geremd," Els Roes, May 16, p. CO4
Arte, "Entorno A Dennis Oppenheim: 1967-1994," Maite Lopez Y Carme Zaera, January, p. 47-49
Arte, "Dennis Oppenheim. El Significado Vertigianoso," Kim Bradley, April-June, 1995, p. 19-24
Cover, Robert C. Morgan, Winter, p. 38
Der Tagesspiegel, "Knockout für die Utopie," Nicola Kuhn, July 8, p. 21
El Tiempo, "Proyectos, viajes y vacios artisticos," José Hernan Aguilar, October 1, p. 11
Kunstforum International, "Light for the Bunker," Justin Hoffmann, August, p. 39
L'Espresso, "Metti l'Arte in Cuffia," Renato Barille, March 24, p. 195
Los Angeles Times, "Going Through the Motions," Cathy Curtis, November 7, p. F-12
Los Angeles Times, "It's Art, Because They Say It's Art," Kristin McKenna, October 8, p.6-7
Munchner Merkur, "Durchs Mundtunnel fahrt die Eisenbahn," Claudia Teibler, October 9, p. 6
Next, "Interview with Dennis Oppenheim," Emma Ercoli, Spring, p. 12-17
OC Weekly, "Machine," Doree Dunlap, November 23, p. 9
Recherches Poetiques, Anne-Francoise Penders, Spring, No. 2, p. 96-113
Rekarte, "Dennis Oppenheim," Marga Perera, March, p. 16
SZ, "Der Horror lauert uberall," Justin Hoffman, October 6, p. 8
Village Voice, "The Age of Ouch," Peter Schjedahl, March 28, p. 10

1996
24 Heures, "A Genève, Dennis Oppenheim fait planer ses menaces sur le MAMCO," Françoise Jaunin, May 7, p. 16
Austin American Statesman, "Still provocative after all this time," Madeline Irvine, February 21, p. E-11
Basler Zeitung, "Die Maschine Mensch," Carole Gurtler, June 3, p. 4
Der Bund, "Die Kunst am Puls der Zeit," Jost Martin Imbach, July 20, p. 2
Der Standard "Opferkerzen für gierige Sammler," Doris Krumpl, November 21, p. A-8
Feuilleton, " Bruckenschlag: Neues in Berliner Kupferstichkabinett," August, p. C-4
Interni, "Da Dennis Oppenheim," Andrea B. Del Guercio, July/August, p. 141-144
Journal de Genève, "Dennis Oppenheim, artiste paysagiste de la pensée humaine," Jean-Pierre Wiittwer, April 11, p. 12
Le Courrier, "Le MAMCO fête le printemps avec une foule d'artistes," Isabelle Bratschi, April 13, p. 11
Liberation, "Oppenheim a la poursuite de lui-meme," Herve Gauville, April 25, p. 5
Next, "Interview with Dennis Oppenheim," Emma Ercoli, Autumn, p. 100-104
Sculpture, "Laumeier Sculpture Park," Jan Garden Castro, November, p. 12-15
Tages Anzeiger, "Schach!-Kunst für die Galle," Von Simon Maurer, April 9, p. 7
The New York Times, Roberta Smith, January 12, p. C-23
Le Nouveau Quotidien, "Avec Dennis Oppenheim, les gens se sentent normaux et la monde parait tres bizarre," Laurent Wolf, p. 6
The San Diego Union Tribune, "Dreaming of Me," Robert L. Pincus, February 11, p. 9
Tribune des Arts, "Genève rend curieusement hommage a Dennis Oppenheim," Etienne Dumont, May, p. 4
Tribune de Genève, "Dennis Oppenheim opere un double retour a la casa zero," Lionel Bavier, March 30, p. 12

1997
Art in America, "Dark Laughter," Eleanor Heartney, April, p. 102-107
Hessische Allgemeine, "Eine Kirche auf dem Kopf," Von Dirk Schwarze, February 27, p. 10

Printed by Amilcare Pizzi Arti grafiche, Cinisello
Balsamo as for Edizioni Charta during June 1997